The Welsh

The Welsh Spirit of Gwent

Mair Elvet Thomas

CARDIFF
UNIVERSITY OF WALES PRESS
1988

British Library Cataloguing in Publication Data

Thomas, Mair Elvet
   The Welsh Spirit of Gwent
   1. Gwent. Welsh culture
   I. Title
   942.9'9

   ISBN 0-7083-1020-6

Typeset in Wales by Megaron, Cardiff
Printed in Wales by Graham Harcourt Printers Ltd., Swansea
Cover design by Cloud Nine, Cardiff

To my brother
Havard Gregory

Contents

	Page
List of Illustrations	viii
Foreword	ix
Cymreigyddion y Fenni	1
The National Eisteddfod in Gwent	13
Printers, Publishers and Authors	45
Poets of Gwent	54
Today and Tomorrow	64

Illustrations

Page

Lady Llanover 6

Lord Tredegar 15

Professor Herkomer 16

Hwfa Môn 16

Sir Ivor Herbert 25

The Gorsedd Circle, Pontypool, 1924 33

Archdruid Elfed, Prosser Rhys and
    Prince Edward at Pontypool, 1924 34

Jennie Lee, Aneurin Bevan and
    Paul Robeson at Ebbw Vale, 1958 41

William Thomas (Islwyn) 59

Edgar Phillips (Tre-fin) 59

Proclamation of the National Eisteddfod,
    Newport, 1987 67

Foreword

The purpose of this book is to show how the Welsh language and Welsh culture have survived in the county of Gwent, one of the most Anglicized of the counties of Wales. Both the present century and the nineteenth reveal its Welsh spirit in different ways, and the nearer we come to the present day the more certain we become that it is alive and thriving. We cannot cease to be amazed that the language has survived against a background of fluctuations in the Welsh-speaking population (owing to economic and other factors), and in spite of the difficulties and frustrations which it has encountered.

Many interesting anecdotes might have been included, especially in Chapter 2, but have been omitted lest the book should become too long. My hope is that what has been told here will inspire as well as inform.

My thanks to Mr John Rhys and members of his staff of the University of Wales Press for their ever-ready advice, to the staff of the Cardiff Central Library reference department, in particular Mr J. Brynmor Jones, for their assistance at all times, and to my well-informed friends in Gwent for much of the contents of the last chapter. I must also remember my patient husband who listened to my many questions and answered them, and my brother who copied my untidy and much altered manuscript on his word processor.

I

Cymreigyddion y Fenni

G WENT has always been part of Wales. By the Act of
Union of 1536, Monmouthshire was formed from lands
on the western side of Offa's Dyke 'in the country of Wales'.
The only difference between Monmouthshire and the other
Welsh shires was that it was under the jurisdiction of the
Oxford Circuit 'for the sake of convenience'. In 1974 the
ancient name Gwent was given to the modern county when
parts of Gwynllŵg (Wentloog) were lost and parts of
Breconshire (Brynmawr and Gilwern) were added.

The Welsh language has experienced a turbulent history in
the county. At one time the nobility — the Herbert, Morgan,
Kemeys and Williams families — were Welsh speaking and
were patrons of famous poets not one of whom was a native
of Gwent. One member of the Morgan family, Ifor ap
Llywelyn, lived in Gwernyclepa, in Basaleg in the fourteenth
century, and he is still known to this day as 'Ifor Hael'
('generous' Ifor), the pseudonym given to him by his bard
and close friend Dafydd ap Gwilym. Two other eminent
fifteenth-century poets, Guto'r Glyn and Lewis Glyn Cothi,
composed poems to members of the Herbert family. Therefore these noblemen must have understood Welsh and
appreciated the works of their bards.

Bishop William Morgan's translation of the Bible into
Welsh in 1588 and the Welsh Book of Common Prayer (1567)
gave an impetus to the Welsh language even though Queen
Elizabeth's intention had been to further the consolidation of
her kingdom through the Protestant religion. Because there
were so many Welsh speakers in Gwent, as in the rest of Wales,
a law was enacted enabling services in Welsh to be held in
churches where it was the language of the congregation.

The common people received no general education till the seventeenth century, when schools were opened by Thomas Gouge and the 'Welsh Trust' to teach poor Welsh children to read and write, to count and to recite the catechism — all in English — to help them to get what was called 'economic advancement' and to serve 'their country' better. In the eighteenth century came the SPCK (the Society for the Promotion of Christian Knowledge) which opened charity schools. They too were biased towards English though they did publish books in Welsh and it is sad to relate that after a while even some of Griffith Jones's renowned circulating schools, which did so much to educate Welsh adults and children, became anglicized in Gwent.

Towards the end of the eighteenth century came the Industrial Revolution. Ironworks and coal-mines were opened, and as these flourished more and more people flocked to Gwent to work. Among them were hundreds of Welsh-speaking folk from south and west Wales bringing with them their language, their traditions, their culture and their Nonconformity. Chapels were built, Welsh societies were formed and the Welsh printing press added its impetus. Indeed, Welsh societies became the order of the day.

The most famous of these societies was founded in Abergavenny. Little did the small group of men who assembled at the Sun Inn on 22 November 1833 imagine that their Cymreigyddion Society, which was launched that night, would draw crowds the size of which had never been seen at an eisteddfod before, and would be prestigious and well-known among scholars in many countries. As the minutes record, they were all 'gentlemen' and 'supporters of the ancient British tongue'. In their next meeting, without more ado, they elected officers from their midst: President, the Revd John Evans, Vicar of Llanover; Vice-President, William Price, Esq., lawyer in Abergavenny; Bard, Mr T.E. Watkins (Eiddil Ifor); Secretary, Mr Thomas Bevan (Caradawc); Correspondent, the Revd Thomas Price, the well-known vicar of Cwm-du and Llangatwg, Breconshire. They all felt that a Welsh Society would be beneficial to the inhabitants of Abergavenny and to those who dwelt 'in the shadow of the mountains of Monmouthshire'. At first the Society followed the pattern of similar Welsh societies scattered over Gwent, holding meetings periodically to discuss business, as well as social and contemporary matters in Wales.

Requests to become members came from several of the gentry, such as Sir Charles Morgan, Tredegar (who soon came to be known as the new Society's 'Ifor Hael') and Mr and Mrs Benjamin Hall and her mother, Mrs Waddington. In a few days, they were joined by Lady Coffin Greenly of Titley Court, Herefordshire (a close friend of Mrs Waddington who could speak Welsh and knew many Welsh folk songs). A catalogue of rules was drawn up, the most important being that every conversation and 'continuous speech' should be carried on 'in Welsh only' — a praiseworthy rule indeed if the Society was to fulfil the purpose and carry out the intention for which it had been founded.

T.E. Watkins was a historian as well as a weigher at the Blaenau Gwent ironworks. Between 1834 and 1837 he won prizes for twelve historical essays in the Society's eisteddfodau. Most of these are still in manuscript in the Cardiff Central Library and the National Library, Aberystwyth; only one — 'Hanes Llanffwyst' (1834) — has seen the light of day, for it was published in 1922 by Bradney and printed at the Minerva Press of the Owen Brothers of Abergavenny. It records that the vast majority of the hills, streams, farms and fields in the parish of Llanffwyst had Welsh names. He wrote another essay on 'The Iron Works of South Wales' which gives particulars of the progress of the Welsh language after their opening. For this fascinating study, Eiddil Ifor gleaned much of his information not from books but from his grandfather who had died in 1812 aged 84 years.

Thomas Bevan (Caradawc or Caradawc y Fenni) was an antiquary engaged in the business of carrying goods on roads and canals. He was born in Breconshire, and while working at the Llanelly works in that county he came into contact with a number of Welshmen interested in Welsh literature. The most notable of these men was the Revd Thomas Price, for it was through his influence that Caradawc came to love Wales

3

and the Welsh language. The fulfilment of his enthusiasm for both Gwent and the language came when Caradawc founded, with others, the Abergavenny Cymreigyddion Society (*Cymdeithas Cymreigyddion y Fenni*). He was its first Secretary and organized its first eisteddfodau which later became 'the event of the year' not only in Gwent but also in Wales.

Although he was not a native of Gwent, the Revd Thomas Price was welcomed with joy by the new society for he was already a well-known national figure. He was a fluent speaker in both Welsh and English, appealed to all classes and possessed a charismatic personality. He had adopted the pseudonym 'Carnhuanawc' since the time he began writing about antiquities to the first popular Welsh paper of the time *Seren Gomer*. And it is by the name Carnhuanawc (Sunny Cairn) that he is known to this day. More than all else, he was an ardent Welshman, and his patriotism was contagious. The patriotism of Carnhuanawc and others like him in the nineteenth century was a cultural patriotism, for they were also loyal to the Queen.

Whenever Carnhuanawc spoke to the Cymreigyddion, he emphasized that Welsh societies like theirs were of no avail unless they advocated education through the medium of Welsh. He even set up a school to do just that. He was one of the enlightened clergy of his day in Wales who attacked the Established Church for appointing English clergy to Welsh parishes and for allowing services in those Welsh parishes to be conducted in English.

But Carnhuanawc's great work is his *Hanes Cymru* which appeared in four parts between 1836 and 1842. It was sold by travelling booksellers, and proved most popular. The author was so eager to tell his fellow men and women about the past glory of their country that he included every scrap of information he could glean, and would not write his book in any other language than Welsh.

In his speeches at the Society's eisteddfodau he never ceased to exhort his audiences to transmit the Welsh language to the next generation, as well as to commend to them and hold up before them important new books published by The Welsh Manuscripts Society formed in 1836 by six of the

Cymreigyddion members (with the Queen as its Patron). Carnhuanawc also praised his audiences for patronizing the Welsh press and told them that cultural standards in Wales were far better than those in England. And his audiences loved him. He was a scholar, although later generations have yet to attribute him his due recognition. As he had done for other eisteddfodau, he spent most of the summer in Llanover planning the 1848 Eisteddfod, although his health was failing. Once more the crowd were thrilled to hear him speak to exhort, to encourage and to praise. In less than a month he was dead. Thus Wales had lost one of its most gifted and beloved sons, and one of its most ardent and practical patriots whose influence for the good of the Welsh language had been immense. *Cymreigyddion y Fenni* was never the same again.

Lady Llanover (when she was Augusta Waddington) came indirectly under his influence early in her life, through her mother's best friend Elizabeth Brown Greenly, later Lady Greenly (or Llwydlas, as she liked to be called), a keen follower of eisteddfodau and a Welsh speaker who had been taught by Carnhuanawc. A composer and singer, she would come to Tŷ Uchaf, Llanover, and sing Welsh folk songs much to the delight of the family and to the young Augusta. It is no wonder that Lady Llanover later became an ardent promoter of these songs. As a child, Augusta played with the Welsh-speaking village children, and always gave her pets Welsh names. She was never as happy anywhere as in Llanover. She first heard Carnhuanawc speak at an eisteddfod in Brecon in 1826 and was inspired by his words extolling the Welsh language, its genius and its power of survival in spite of great difficulties. From that day a friendship of kindred spirits developed between them which lasted for over twenty years.

In 1834 there was an eisteddfod in Cardiff where she won first prize for an essay on the advantages deriving from keeping the Welsh language and the Welsh costume. She used the *nom de plume* 'Gwenynen Gwent' (the Bee of Gwent) by which she became known for the rest of her life. Promoting Welsh culture, the triple harp, Welsh folk-singing and the Welsh woollen industry became the most important of her interests. She and her husband, Sir Benjamin Hall, built a

Augusta Waddington Hall, Lady Llanover (1802–1867).
(Painting by C.A. Mornewicke: private collection.
Photography: National Museum of Wales.)

large house and called it Llys Llanofer (Llanover Court) which became a centre for Welsh culture.

Lord and Lady Llanover's families and family connections supported the Cymreigyddion Society. Sir Benjamin was a member of the Crawshay family of Merthyr Tudful, through his mother. Amongst other family friends were the Guests and especially the Morgan family of Tredegar.

Sir Charles Morgan sent a letter to the Society as soon as it was established expressing his wish to become a member and he was most generous in his contributions. We find the names of other noble families of Gwent among the patrons, presidents and donors of prizes. Thus was formed a network of gentry who, during the first half of the nineteenth century, supported Welsh in Gwent. It may have been because they felt that such Welsh institutions kept the Welsh people peaceful when the Chartists were campaigning for the rights of the common people and when there were uprisings in other European countries. If so, they also had to recognize that this particular Society and others like it in Gwent were also helping to promote the Welsh language and to enhance the dignity of the Welsh-speaking inhabitants in their county.

Lady Llanover employed Welsh-speaking servants and gave Welsh names to them and to their particular work. She had her own Welsh chaplain and kept an official harpist. She, together with others, revived many of the old folk songs. And she gave every place she could on her estate a Welsh name. In the National Library is a collection of paintings by her showing the women's costumes of some of the Welsh districts, including Gwent. Through the efforts of Lady Llanover and Carnhuanawc, the triple harp became the national instrument of the eisteddfodau during the nineteenth century, until the piano, much to her disgust, replaced it. She even opened a factory in Llanover to make and repair harps.

She was unique in her day. There was no woman in Gwent, nor in the rest of Wales, more enthusiastic than she for the Welsh language, although she was neither able to speak it at all well nor write it unaided. Encouraged and supported by her husband, she did her best for Welsh culture in her corner of Wales when it was the fashion among her class to deride and despise both the language and those who spoke it.

The Halls were 'well-to-do' and so could buy books and papers in Welsh and in English on things Welsh, adding to them regularly, thus amassing a huge library at Llanover. They were also able to buy Iolo Morganwg's manuscripts from his son, and over seventy volumes of them are now housed in the National Library. When their only son died, Welsh was given pride of place on his grave. The same was done when Lord Llanover died in 1867, and this was continued on Gwenynen Gwent's death in 1896. The mausoleum in Llanover churchyard is a fitting memorial to them both.

Her brother-in-law, Christian Charles Josias Bunsen, was a famous German scholar and linguist. He was also a friend of Prince Albert, the Queen's Consort. While he was German ambassador in London, he showed a deep interest in the Cymreigyddion Society. He knew the German scholars of the day and the subjects in which they were interested. So he encouraged the Society to set the subjects which would entice them to compete. And this happened in 1838, 1840 and 1842. The prize of £84 offered in 1840 was won by a German, Albert Schulz, for an essay on 'The effect which Welsh Traditions have had on the Literature of Germany, France and Scandinavia'. An essay in Welsh on a similar subject had been awarded a much smaller prize in 1836; it was by David Lewis, from Blaenau, and remains in manuscript in Cardiff Central Library. In 1838, John Dorney Harding of Rockfield, Monmouthshire, Queen's Advocate, was awarded the main prize by the medieval historian, Henry Hallam, who adjudicated his work. This was the period when Charlotte Guest was busy translating the *Mabinogion* into English with assistance from a number of Welshmen, among them Carnhuanawc.

The German scholars were also intensely interested in the Celtic languages at this time; so in 1842 the biggest prize was given for an essay dealing with the place of Welsh among the Celtic languages 'and together with the other branches of the same, among the languages of the Indo-European races'. The subject was patriotic and contemporary and would go far to promote knowledge of the origins of the Welsh language. Once again, a German, Carl Meyer, won the prize. It is said that he went on to learn Welsh with the help of Carnhuanawc and others. Thus the Society showed that it was progressive, and, with the help of Bunsen, made Welsh known on the continent, giving it a dignified status amongst the languages of Europe.

However, those essays did nothing to promote the Welsh language in Gwent. It was among ordinary people that the language was promoted — among those who wrote their essays in Welsh and tried to compose poems in Welsh, though neither did the subjects of many of the poetry competitions arouse much inspiration nor was the standard of the compositions remarkable. But the ordinary Welsh people tried when circumstances were militating against them — long working hours, little money, lack of education in Welsh, bad housing, gross unfairness on all hands. Some poets of a higher calibre also competed, but even their compositions are not acknowledged amongst their works as having lasting value. One great poet among them, however — Islwyn — will be dealt with in a later chapter, together with his association with *Cymreigyddion y Fenni*.

There is one other name connected with the Cymreig-yddion Society that cannot be ignored: Thomas Stephens of Merthyr Tudful (1821–75). He was not a native of Gwent, nor did he live at any time in Gwent; but it was the ninth eisteddfod in Abergavenny, in 1848, which gave him his chance, for the principal essay that year was 'A critical Essay on the History of the Language and Litcrature of Wales during the twelfth and two successive centuries; containing numerous specimens of Ancient Welsh Poetry in the original; and accompanied with English translations'. The prize was £25 given by Queen Victoria in the name of the Prince of Wales. The winner was already well-known in his home town and had competed in the Abergavenny eisteddfodau of 1840 and 1845. But his critical essay in 1848 brought him instant, unqualified fame, for the adjudicator, the Venerable John Williams, Archdeacon of Cardiganshire, announced that a new star had appeared 'in the firmament of Welsh Literature'. The essay was as unique as the donor of the prize, and the crowd was electrified when they saw a young man who was but twenty-seven years of age get to his feet in answer to his pseudonym. The adjudicator proclaimed that the essay should be published without delay, which prompted Josiah John Guest to say at once that he would pay the cost. The book was printed by William Rees of Llandovery and published by him and Longman & Co, London, the following year as *The Literature of the Kymry*. Its author became known far and wide as a scholar, on the Continent and in Australia and America. Though *Cymreigyddion y Fenni* accomplished a great deal of important work, this is its greatest, namely setting the subject and giving Stephens the opportunity to establish a wide recognition and readership. For the rest of the nineteenth century the name of the Society was linked with this one book which was the authority on the period in the history of Welsh literature, covered in such a scientific way in Thomas Stephens' essay — the only book he ever published. Other works by him remain in manuscript form in the National Library.

The minutes of the Society are among its manuscripts in the National Library and they, of course, reveal the Welshness of the Society. Of the minutes kept by the four secretaries, those kept by the first two are the most interesting for their neatness, accuracy and detail. At first they kept them in Welsh only, but in November 1837 it was decided that they should be bilingual in order to please the members in general, so that all could understand them and be informed about the activities of the Society. The desire was also expressed that this would encourage those who did not understand Welsh to learn it. The public meetings of the Society had already become bilingual because many of the members who attended them did not understand Welsh — nor did all the visitors and patrons. Lady Llanover made sure that those ladies among the patrons who understood no Welsh at least wore the Welsh costume at the eisteddfodau, thus advertising the new patterns and colours of the Welsh materials. However, while these ladies may have looked 'completely

Welsh', we are told that some of them 'to their sorrow', were ignorant of the ancient Welsh language. Ieuan ap Gruffydd took over the secretaryship of the society in 1839 when the minutes were bilingual. A schoolmaster at Llanwenarth and an ardent Welshman, he deplored the apathy and lack of zeal and patriotism among the members who attended the meetings in Abergavenny between the eisteddfodau, for they would only smoke and listen to the harp and not engage in any activity which meant using Welsh. So Ieuan decided of his own accord, once and for all, that the minutes at least would henceforth be in Welsh only. He ends his lament in English so that all who read it could understand his intention:

> . . . as we are all *Cymreigyddion*, I shall enter the same [i.e., the minutes] in the Ancient British Language, and that only, and let those who wish to read, and does [*sic*] not understand that Language, learn it.

We are not told whether there was any disapproval, and Ieuan proceeds to write the minutes in detail in his inimitable, picturesque Welsh. The last two secretaries reverted to English only, with no effort to keep a regular account of the meetings held. Indeed, the impression one receives is that there was nothing of any importance to record between the eisteddfodau. These were public 'shows' and drew thousands of people from far and wide to see the coaches of the gentry with their visitors from foreign lands. There had never been such processions — of bards dressed in their robes and wearing their insignia, of waggons carrying women in Welsh costumes spinning and weaving, men engaged in printing programmes and throwing them to the crowds before the ink had dried, and young girls playing harps. The town was swathed in bunting, flowers and greenery and banners in honour of the Welsh language and the Eisteddfod, and paying allegiance to Queen Victoria. The hall where the proceedings were held could never contain all who wished to enter to take part and to listen. Bands played, church bells rang. Inside the Cymreigyddion Hall was gas lighting, a huge banner with the letters V R, flowers and greenery, and two platforms — one for the harpists with their triple harps, and one for the gentry, their guests and speakers. The audiences inside and the crowds outside were enthralled, and not once in the accounts of the immense crowds and of the eisteddfod proceedings was any accident or other catastrophe recorded. Yet, on 14 January 1854, when the committee met, it was decided, at the Chairman's behest, without any warning and with no reason given, that 'the Abergavenny Cymmrigiddion [*sic*] Society be this day dissolved'. The Secretary must have been deeply moved to make such a mistake in the spelling of the Society's name, for he was the Revd John Evans of Llanover, its first President.

2

The National Eisteddfod in Gwent

T HE first National Eisteddfod was held in Aberdare in
1861, a year after it was decided to hold National
Eisteddfodau. From 1861 to 1868, an Eisteddfod was held
annually. However, during the following years lack of funds
prevented the National Eisteddfod being held until 1881,
when it took place in Merthyr Tudful. Since that year, except
for two breaks during the First and Second World Wars the
National Eisteddfod has been held every year, alternating
between north and south Wales. Four have been held in
Gwent — at Newport (Casnewydd) in 1897, at Abergavenny
(Y Fenni) in 1913, at Pontypool (Pont-y-pŵl) in 1924, and at
Ebbw Vale (Glynebwy) in 1958.

Each offered Welsh culture, drew large crowds and had its
own particular character. Local committees were formed to
deal with different aspects of the work involved, and all
worked together amicably for quite a long time in order to
make the eisteddfodau a success, and in its time each was a
success. As the years went by the use of Welsh improved.
There was a remarkable number of eminent men — and an
increasing number of women — in the lists of presidents,
guarantors, patrons and adjudicators: people who were
involved in education, music, poetry and prose and in the arts
in Wales. Over the years the names changed, but there was no
less enthusiasm for the Eisteddfod, its aims and its success.
Each occasion made the people of Gwent conscious of a
language and a culture that should not die.

The 1897 Eisteddfod

The Eisteddfod of 1897 was held in Newport. The first day
was devoted to bands and choirs, each day had its presidents,

and there were two stage conductors, who took it in turn to keep order in the pavilion and to ensure that all went according to plan. The Eisteddfod choir boasted 500 voices, and the orchestra 100 instrumentalists; there were official singers, two official harpists, a pianist and accompanists. In some ways, the pattern of events was similar to the present day, but in reality there is a vast difference between the Newport National Eisteddfod of 1897 and the Eisteddfod held there over ninety years later in 1988.

The printed programme of the Eisteddfod was largely bilingual with the exception of the list of the publications which was in Welsh. The descriptions of all the competitions at the Newport Eisteddfod were bilingual, even the Arts and Science section, as were the conditions and rules for the competitors. Most of the advertisements were in English only and bilingual if they advertised any activities connected with the Eisteddfod. However, the pharmaceutical firm, Boots, placed a very prominent advertisement on two whole pages of the programme — one side in Welsh and the opposite page in English. The Honourable Society of Cymmrodorion also included a bilingual advertisement. The Society's secretary from 1888 onwards, Vincent Evans, was also secretary of the Eisteddfod Association, and from 1881 the editor of its publications. An influential man in Welsh circles in London and in Wales, he brought order to the Eisteddfod's various activities and to its finances.

The names recorded in the official programme of those who were members of the various committees in 1897 are legion — people in Newport and the surrounding areas who took a practical interest in the most important Welsh institution which had come to such an Anglicized county as Monmouthshire. The list of guarantors is also a long one. The President, Lord Tredegar was prominent in the county's social, industrial and educational institutions. He, the Marquis of Bute (a scholar and president of the Rhyl Eisteddfod in 1890), Lord Windsor (a member of the Plymouth family of St Fagans) and Sir Clifford Cory (one of the sons of the great philanthropist John Cory and Anna Maria, daughter of the Newport coalowner John Beynon) all

Lord Tredegar, President of the National Eisteddfod of Wales 1897.
(*By permission of Newport Museum and Art Gallery.*)

The Archdruid, Hwfa Môn.
(*By permission of Newport Museum and Art Gallery.*)

Professor Herkomer.
(*By permission of Newport Museum and Art Gallery.*)

subscribed generously and attended, but could not speak the language. Another of the distinguished presidents was the Celtic scholar Sir John Rhŷs who also contributed an invaluable service to Welsh education and culture, and was a pioneer in many fields of learning.

The pavilion could hold 10,000 people when used to capacity and, with the audience free to enter and leave at will, the voices of the two well-known conductors, Mabon and Cynonfardd, were essential in maintaining order. Mabon was William Abraham, MP for the Rhondda, and first president of the South Wales Miners' Federation. He had a penetrating voice and became a most popular conductor of eisteddfodau during the end of the nineteenth and beginning of the twentieth century. He was also among those who founded the first Welsh Language Society in 1885; the first society to oppose the Government's policy of insisting that English be the only language used in schools. Cynonfardd, the Revd Thomas Edwards, had emigrated to America but in 1897 was brought back to conduct the Newport Eisteddfod.

The Gorsedd of Bards was held on three mornings — Tuesday, Thursday and Friday — and drew large crowds. There was a procession of notables to the 'Sacred Circle' preceded by policemen on horseback and with policemen on foot mingling with the procession. The Archdruid, Hwfa Môn (the Revd Rowland Williams), was a chaired and crowned bard in the National Eisteddfod. And it must be recorded that the only section of the National Eisteddfod of Wales which was wholy conducted in Welsh at that time was the Gorsedd of the Bards.

In 1897 the bards were attired in new outfits designed by Professor Herkomer and given for their use as a gift 'for ever'. Lord Tredegar had a model of the *Corn Hirlas*, or Horn of Plenty, which the young artist Goscombe John had designed with appropriate silver adornments and which Lord Tredegar eventually presented to the Gorsedd. That very same horn is still used and will be used at the Newport Eisteddfod this year (1988) — ninety years later.

In the ceremony held on the Thursday, Tom Ellis, Lloyd George and R.A. Griffith were received into the Gorsedd.

Ellis adopted the bardic name 'Cynlas'; he had been Liberal Member of Parliament for Merionethshire since 1896, and was a supporter of Home Rule for Wales, Church Disestablishment and Land Reform. David Lloyd George, of course, needs little introduction; he adopted the bardic name 'Llwyd o Wynedd' (Lloyd of Gwynedd), had been MP for the Caernarfonshire Boroughs since 1890 and at the beginning of his career had championed the same causes as Tom Ellis. Robert Arthur Griffith (Elphin), was a lawyer and an author, as well as an enthusiastic frequenter of eisteddfodau. He was prominent and influential for a period as a poet, a dramatist, critic and reviewer. One of his plays, a satire on eisteddfod activities of the day, had been published in a Welsh periodical as early as 1895 and is acclaimed as the best by far of the plays written in Welsh at the end of the nineteenth century. He also won a prize for the best play at the Newport Eisteddfod of 1897.

Most of the literary and poetry competitions had, naturally, a distinct Welsh flavour, and therefore the majority had to be written in Welsh. There were poetry competitions in free verse and in the traditional classic metres for which there are no equivalent English terms (*awdl, englyn, hir a thoddaid, cywydd*). The subjects offered were 'From Anglesey to Monmouthshire', 'The Beehive', 'The Banks of the Usk', 'In memory of Daniel Owen' (who had died in 1895), an elegy to the late Lord Aberdare (who had also died in 1895) and to Gwenynen Gwent (who died in 1896), a satirical poem 'Football Worship' and a play about 'The Massacre of Abergavenny'.

Some prose competitions showed the literary committee's awareness of their county's history: for example, an 'Account of the Welsh dialects of Gwent and Morgannwg'; a 'Collection of Gwent folklore'; and a 'Dictionary of Welsh names of rivers and places in Monmouthshire' (including Welsh field names). The committee must have felt deeply that the children of Welsh parents were not given a fair deal in the schools; so it set an essay on the best means of preserving and teaching Welsh among children of Welsh parents in English-speaking districts. An essay on the advantages of education in

Art and Science to the working class in Wales was to be written in Welsh only. There was also a competition for novels, to be written in English in 13–26 parts, suitable for publication weekly.

The Crowning of the Bard ceremony took place on the Wednesday, when there were several thousands of people in the pavilion, and the names of those assembled on the platform are given in full in the Welsh report in *Baner ac Amserau Cymru* (The Banner and Times of Wales). The Archdruid (Hwfa Môn) made his appearance last of all (draped in his new colourful robes and carrying the sword) to the great enthusiasm of the audience. Sir John Rhŷs, during this ceremony, used his presidential address to bring pressure on the Welsh MPs to secure justice for Wales. The crowned bard was a Welsh Congregational minister in Blaenafon, T. Mafonwy Davies. He was adjudicated the best of nine who had composed an epic poem on 'Arthur of the Round Table'. Two of the adjudicators were to become Archdruids, namely Dyfed and Elfed. The chair was won on Thursday by J.T. Job, a Welsh Calvinistic Methodist minister in Aberdare: this was his first success of many at winning the chair. One of his adjudicators, Pedrog, also became Archdruid. Both the crown and the chair poems were comprehensive works which covered every aspect of their subjects: this was the eisteddfodic tradition. Today they would have little merit, and nothing in them has been of any real value as poetry. They merely conformed to the fashion of the day and to what was expected of the poets who wrote such works.

All the adjudications were delivered from the platform with the winners going up to receive their awards. The music, arts and science adjudications were in English. Some of the literary adjudicators were outstanding Welshmen in their day and contributed to Wales in many ways. Their names reflect the astuteness of the literary committee members and their desire to bring some of the prominent men of Wales to their Eisteddfod. Owen Morgan Edwards, later Sir Owen M. Edwards, was an editor and a litterateur as well as an educationist. His influence on the Welsh educational system was tremendous when that system was geared to English.

When he came to the 1897 Eisteddfod he had been Fellow and History Tutor at Lincoln College, Oxford, since 1889, and had written many books of value. He had also established his two influential periodicals — *Cymru* and *Cymru'r Plant*. Colonel, later Sir, Joseph Bradney, was an Englishman who learned Welsh and is best known as the historian of Monmouthshire. Ernest Rhys was a poet, a novelist and an editor, known widely as the General Editor of *The Everyman Library*. William Edwards was Principal and Professor of New Testament Greek at Pontypool Baptist College, and continued as Principal on its removal to Cardiff. Sir John Williams was the chief benefactor of the National Library of Wales, and he was Queen Victoria's doctor. He donated an immense wealth of manuscripts to the Library on condition that it would be located in Aberystwyth. John Gwenogfryn Evans was a paleographer and editor of Welsh manuscripts. His first volume of *Old Welsh Texts* was published in 1887. All his work is valuable because of the minute correctness of his reading from the manuscripts.

The 1897 Eisteddfod received mixed reports in the press. It was recorded that the pavilion was only half-full for the chairing ceremony on the Thursday and that the enthusiasm was very mild; indeed the correspondent for the Welsh paper *Baner ac Amserau Cymru* said that he did not remember such a remarkably tame chairing and one so lacking in curiosity, a situation distinct from the full pavilion and captive audience for the bands and choirs. However, there had been a much larger gathering at the crowning ceremony on the Tuesday.

A well-known figure amongst the music adjudicators was John Thomas (Pencerdd Gwalia, 'The Chief Musician of Wales'), Queen Victoria's official harpist. In 1838, when only twelve years of age, he won the prize of a triple harp at the Abergavenny Eisteddfod, and by the 1897 Eisteddfod had already collected four volumes of Welsh tunes and had edited *Songs of Wales* in 1874. He was known in London, Rome and Florence and had composed many pieces for previous eisteddfodau. David Emlyn Evans, another music adjudicator, was a much younger man, but he too had won many prizes in eisteddfodau, mainly for compositions, including extended choral works. He edited and harmonized over 500 traditional Welsh airs and published them as *Alawon fy Ngwlad* ('My Country's Airs'). Sadly he died at the beginning of 1913 before the Abergavenny Eisteddfod of that year.

In the main, the evening concerts were held in English, and among the items presented was the first performance of 'The Battle of the Severn' by D.C. Williams of Merthyr, which was received with warmth and acclaim by audience and critics. In the concert at the end of the first day, military bands from England performed, and the outstanding item was a Grand Fantasia on the life story of the Queen entitled 'VR'. At the end of each concert the audience sang the English National Anthem, while *Hen Wlad fy Nhadau* ended all the proceedings in the pavilion. Clara Butt, the famous English contralto, sang in English on the platform during one of the ceremonies and also sang her encore in English.

In contrast to the more traditional musical events, a competition was held for an ambitious architectural project — a plan for a National Museum and Art Gallery for Wales, the cost to be no more than £20,000. The prize was won by John Bain of Newport. On the Friday, the last day of the Eisteddfod, Lord Kenyon speaking about the future National Museum and where it might be located, and about the difficulty of securing the necessary finance from the Treasury, suggested that the Eisteddfod bring its influence to bear on the issue.

Baner ac Amserau Cymru reported favourably on a speech in Welsh by Dean Howell (Llawdden) of St David's. According to the report, it was a powerful speech, characteristic of him and consistent with 'the old eisteddfodic institution'. A likeable character and an eloquent Welsh speaker, he received a rousing reception; every heart warmed to Llawdden as he spoke in clear, pure and unaffected Welsh. Nothing like it had been heard for many years: without a doubt it was one of the highlights of the Newport Eisteddfod of 1897.

It is important not to be unduly critical of the 1897 Eisteddfod: it followed the pattern of eisteddfodau held in regions far more Welsh than Newport and its environs. The

'Welsh only' rule was yet to come, and much of the competitions and work submitted by the poets and litterateurs followed the same rules and regulations as for other eisteddfodau. At that time, there was no *Pabell Lên* (Literature Pavilion); so all the adjudications — most of them in English — were delivered from the pavilion platform. Welsh speakers and non-Welsh speakers alike were equally enthusiastic and anxious that the eisteddfodau held in Gwent should be as great a success as possible. Those held in Gwent in the twentieth century actively brought change for the better, as will be seen in the remainder of this chapter.

The 1913 Eisteddfod

The 1913 Eisteddfod was far livelier and more Welsh-conscious than the Newport event of the previous century. The Gorsedd was one hundred per cent Welsh, and more speakers were aware of the importance of Welsh in education, in the Eisteddfod itself, in drama and in music. However although the official list of subjects, prizes and conditions, and the official programme of the Abergavenny Eisteddfod, were full, interesting and detailed, they contained little Welsh. The vast majority of the advertisements were in English only. A few were bilingual and very few indeed in Welsh only, which suggests that businesses did not consider Welsh to be a commercial language. Even the leading article which gave an account of the literary associations of Abergavenny was in English only. A prominent feature was the large number of advertisements for beer and other drinks. The programme contained a formidable list of guarantors from Abergavenny and full, long lists of the people who were involved in the various local committees. The lists of subjects, prizes and conditions were bilingual (Welsh subjects in Welsh only) except for the Art, Science and Industry section which was wholly in English, as were the entry forms for all competitions. *Penillion* singing was introduced for the first time in Gwent, and harp solos on triple and pedal harps, and also compositions to Welsh words. Some of the architecture and design competitions seem particularly interesting (e.g., designs for a Welsh village institute and library, for a

Welsh Christmas card, and for a bardic chair). There were also a wide variety of craft competitions to attract non-Welsh speakers. In the schools' section every item was in English.

The pavilion, constructed in Bailey Park at a cost of £1,560, was made in all its detail (except for the gas lighting) in Abergavenny itself. The opening day began with a Pageant of Gwent in the grounds of Maindiff Court, near Abergavenny, depicting 'the history of the Eisteddfod and of the principal leaders of Gwent from the coming of the Cymry to the reign of Charles I' in twelve episodes. It proved to be a huge success with almost 12,000 spectators on the field and thousands having to be turned away. The pageant was being tried as a solution to the customary poor attendance on previous opening days with the bands, ambulance competitions and military tournaments. Indeed there was a general feeling that those activities did not fit in with the spirit of the national festival. But this pageant with its 'kaleidoscopic effect, dramatic presentation and despatch with which episodes followed each other' (as the *Western Mail*'s special correspondent reported in the paper the following day) was altogether different. Even if it was all in English, except for the Welsh names of the characters, the pageant was thoroughly Welsh in spirit and proved so popular that it was hoped other Eisteddfodau might emulate it in the future. It had entailed enormous expense and a great deal of sacrifice on the part of all the actors, for all 800 had paid for their own costumes. Many of the county families joined in and it seems that every Gwent band was there. Indeed every section of the community was involved. There was an episode in which Elizabeth I was presented with a Welsh Bible by Mistress Scudamore; another in lighter vein with Dafydd ap Gwilym and his patron Ifor Hael; one about Gwladys Gam, immortalized by Lewis Glyn Cothi as 'the star of Abergavenny'; and a dramatization of the base murder of Seisyllt ap Dyfnwal and other Welsh chieftains in Abergavenny castle by William de Braose, the fifth lord of the castle. The organizers of the pageant knew the history of their county, and all the performers impressed the audience by their obvious enjoyment.

The repeat performance clashed with the evening concert, but that did not prevent a high attendance at the latter. The concert was made possible through the generosity of Lord Howard de Walden who had contributed £200 towards the expenses of a professional orchestra. With the exception of Mendelssohn's 'Fingal's Cave' the whole evening was devoted to Welsh composers. Pencerdd Gwalia, who had died the previous March, was remembered by his harp solo 'Fantasia'. The highlight of the performance was Joseph Holbrooke's concerto for piano and orchestra, 'The Song of Gwyn ap Nudd'.

The same evening at a Cymmrodorion meeting two papers were read, by Llewelyn Williams, KC, MP, and R.A. Griffith (Elphin). The former declared that the drama of the Welsh people should be as distinctly Welsh as the work of Dafydd ap Gwilym or Ceiriog. Its genius should be Welsh and it should draw its inspiration not merely from the social life of the day but from the traditions and legends of the past. Elphin was a playwright himself and his stirring paper on 'The prospects of Welsh Drama', drawing from his own experience, was full of humour. The Welshman, he said, was inherently dramatic in whatever he did. Never was he more theatrical than when he donned bardic robes and entered the mystic circle of the Gorsedd; there might be greater poets than Hwfa Môn, the former Archdruid, but there was no finer actor. There was among the Welsh a mine of humanity — a 'Klondyke waiting for the prospector and the digger'. The Welsh character was too complex for a cursory study which seemed to have been the case in the so-called contemporary novels. He criticized the dramas of the Eisteddfod as merely preparatory exercises which counted for nothing as literature. He recommended that their authors should study Ibsen, for the situation in Norway in Ibsen's day was similar to that of Wales in the early twentieth century. Welsh drama should not be 'contaminated by the lubricity of the French casino' nor by the 'indecent puerilities of the London music halls'.

Everything augured well for a magnificent Eisteddfod. The weather was bright, warm and fine, and the district was one of the most attractive and beautiful in Wales. The town

Sir Ivor Herbert, grandson of Lady Llanover.
(*By permission of the National Library of Wales.*)

with its 9,000 inhabitants had an atmosphere of welcome and enthusiasm, for was not the district associated with a renaissance in Welsh literature during the mid-nineteenth century when the Cymreigyddion did such excellent work and brought scholars and other eminent people from far afield to its eisteddfodau? On the morning of 4 August the town had a military air with 3,000 men belonging to the London Scottish Regiment, the Queen's Westminster Rifles and the Fourth London Battalion parading through the streets.

There was a full programme every day for the four days from 5 to 8 August and a concert every night. An influx of Welsh people was expected for the crowning and chairing ceremonies, but the largest crowds would come to hear the choirs, though set pieces were still mostly English. The Gorsedd ceremony was held on three mornings after members had marched in procession through the streets with full regalia. For the afternoon ceremonies a supreme effort was made to keep to a time schedule on the pavilion platform, despite the short times allotted for competitors and adjudicators. The Eisteddfod stage conductors must have had a difficult time supervising the competitors on the platform and controlling the crowd in the pavilion who kept milling to and fro. As in 1897, Cynonfardd was one of the conductors along with Llew Tegid and Llew Meirion. They must have adopted the pseudonym 'Llew' (Lion) because of their need to raise their voices to an occasional roar to make themselves heard. This was the period of the suffragettes; so, in order to avoid any possible disturbance, more police were stationed around the field and in the town, but their presence was unnecessary.

At the Gorsedd ceremony in the Grove on the Thursday, Sir Ivor Herbert, grandson of Lord and Lady Llanover, was invested as a member with the pseudonym 'Eryr Gwent' (The Eagle of Gwent), along with women who were Welsh authors — Moelona and Eluned, the former from Wales, the latter from Patagonia. As part of the ceremony, Eos Dâr, one of the Gorsedd singers, sang these defiant words to harp accompaniment from the *Maen Llog* (Logan Stone):

Nis gall Lloegr gyda'i rhodres
Wneuthur Mynwy byth yn Saesnes;
Rhaid yw chwalu'r bryniau'n yfflon
Cyn y gellir mynd â'i chalon.

(England with her pomp can never make Monmouthshire English; the hills must be shattered into smither-
eens before her heart can be taken away.)

During the ceremony the Archdruid carried a sceptre and
some of the bards wore their chains of office which had been
presented to the Gorsedd by the Vicar of Bexley, Kent, the
Revd C.E. Wright (Carwr Cymru, 'Lover of Wales'), who
had taken a great deal of interest in the eisteddfodau for quite
a time. He was an invalid and sat in a chair near the *Maen Llog*
and was himself decorated with a chain by the Archdruid.
These insignia are still worn by the Gorsedd officials. Sir
Ivor Herbert spoke in Welsh and referred to the mountains,
rivers, brooks, woods, rocks and all that had endured from
generation to generation, proclaiming their Welshness in
their names. Lord Pontypridd had already spoken praising
the Eisteddfod for what it had done for Wales, for it had been
Wales's university for centuries. He trusted that the new
University of Wales would work together with the Eisteddfod, for the leaders of one were the leaders of the other.

In the chairing ceremony on the Thursday, the chaired
bard was a Welsh and Science master at Merthyr Tudful
Municipal School, T.J. Thomas, better known by his bardic
name 'Sarnicol'. He had already published a number of
volumes of poetry and had won many prizes at eisteddfodau.
His *awdl* was on the subject 'Yr Aelwyd Gymraeg' ('The
Welsh Hearth'). The pavilion was crowded, in anticipation of
the speaker, Lloyd George, who was at the time Chancellor of
the Exchequer. To the dismay and disappointment of the
crowd he was unable to come because of pressure of work
before the parliamentary recess. Sarnicol was a native of
Cardiganshire as was the crowned bard, William Evans, (Wil
Ifan), a minister from Bridgend who was not yet a member of
the Gorsedd. The band, as usual, played 'See, the Con-
quering Hero Comes' as the bard was led to the platform!

The Archdruid of Brittany also visited the Gorsedd during this Eisteddfod. The Gorsedd stones were placed on Rhiw Yspytty where the procession of bards at the Cymreigyddion eisteddfodau used to go out to meet the visitors and the gentry in their carriages. (Five Bretons had visited the 1838 Eisteddfod when one of them, La Villemarqué, was received into the Gorsedd.) Sir Ivor Herbert (who became Lord Treowen in 1917) paid tribute to his grandmother, Lady Llanover, and wished the Eisteddfod every success and the language and nation *hir oes* ('long life'). Lord Howard de Walden disclosed that he was learning Welsh and that he dearly hoped to be able to speak it. The Eisteddfod song, 'Hoff Wlad fy Ngenedigaeth' ('The Dear Land of my Birth'), was sung by Tom Bonnell and the audience sang the hymn tune 'Aberystwyth', led by John Owen y Fenni, in honour of Lord Howard.

Some of the literature competitions — both poetry and prose — at the Eisteddfod were interesting and are worthy of mention. It is clear that there was an improvement in the standard of the competitors as well as in the subjects offered. For instance, six entries for the crown were well within reach of the prize. Despite this, some prizes were withheld, but nevertheless the subjects on the whole were more congenial than in 1897. A Welsh Congregational minister in Llanelli, Gwylfa Roberts, won the prize for his sonnet on 'Tintern Abbey'. A competition for a satirical poem on 'The Pedant' was won by E. Morgan Humphreys, a young journalist and novelist in Caernarfon who was one of the first authors to realize that suitable reading matter in Welsh was sorely needed for young people in order to counteract the flood of English books. He himself wrote excellent books for them. The prize of £15 for a metrical drama in Welsh or English and suitable for stage production, on the life of William Herbert, first Earl of Pembroke, was won by R. Stephens of Pontypool.

The subjects of the essay and handbook competitions had a local flavour — a Bibliographical Dictionary of Notable Men and Women of Gwent on the lines of *Enwogion Ceredigion*, 1869 ('Famous People of Cardiganshire') by Gwynionydd

(Benjamin Williams), who was at one time vicar of Llanover; a critical essay on the works and genius of Islwyn, and another on Thomas Stephens, author of *The Literature of the Kymry* (1849); a social study of any district in Wales; essays on colliery developments and on farming in Monmouthshire; and a collection of placenames in Monmouthshire and adjoining counties. There were also competitions for translation from English and Latin into Welsh and from Welsh into English (specified hymns by Ann Griffiths).

Other competitions included recitations in Welsh: 'Y Ffoadur' ('The Fugitive') by Cynonfardd, a highly dramatic piece which used the voice and theatrical poses fashionable in elocution at the time and for children a scene from Daniel Owen's novel *Rhys Lewis* — 'Ymweliad Thomas Bartley â'r Bala' ('Thomas Bartley's visit to Bala').

The meetings of the various societies during the week are revealing because the speeches delivered in them reflect the many problems facing the Welsh language at the time. A Conference of the League of Welsh Societies, chaired by Sir Edward Anwyl, felt that it was necessary to unite the numerous Welsh societies in Wales. A Celtic scholar and Professor of Welsh in the University College of Wales, Aberystwyth, he died in 1914 before beginning his appointment as Principal of Caerleon Training College.

The Revd Tywi Jones, editor of the popular radical newspaper *Y Darian*, addressed the conference on the need for a league to protect the traditions of Wales. Mr Roland Thomas of Brecon maintained that the Welsh Bible was nearer the original Hebrew than the English Bible owing to the power of the Welsh language to reproduce the deep religious fervour of the Hebrew language. He also asserted that Welsh hymnology was unrivalled as an expression of the spiritual experience of a whole people. He maintained that the language problem arose because of the influx of people from beyond Offa's Dyke into Wales which created a social problem when English-speaking people attended the church services. Another speaker, from Cardiff, Dewi Fychan, pointed out that there had been a decline in the proportion of those who were monoglot Welsh speakers, and that there had been a continual decline in church membership. He urged Welsh people to exert themselves on behalf of the language and its literature. Much had been lost to Wales by the 'natural courtesy' of the Welsh in speaking broken English to please the minority of English people who might be present at a meeting. This courtesy had been abused and, as a result, it had developed into a distinct weakness.

During his presidential address, Major-General Sir Francis Lloyd proclaimed that it was sacrilege to speak English at the Eisteddfod. He was proud that he, a soldier, had been received into the Gorsedd, and called to mind the soldiers Llywelyn, Dafydd Gam and Owain Glyndŵr. He told his audience to promote the culture and freedom of Wales and all things which worked for the good of the country among the nations.

At the Welsh Bibliographical Society's meeting, Colonel Bradney read a paper on 'Rare and Early Printed Books relating to Monmouthshire'. The manuscripts of Iolo Morganwg were discussed, and grateful thanks given to Lady Llanover and her daughter, Mrs Herbert, for realizing their great worth and keeping them so well preserved.

Again can be seen the important contribution another Eisteddfod in Gwent made to Welsh life and culture. The Abergavenny Eisteddfod became a discussion platform and an integral part of the Welsh national scene.

The 1924 Eisteddfod

Eleven years later, the National Eisteddfod came to Gwent for the third time. Pontypool was a fortunate choice for the location — a fairly modern town, situated in the heart of the county with a mixture of agriculture and industry. John Capel Hanbury, one of the nobility of the area, had presented to the town a lovely deer park in which the Eisteddfod was held from 4 to 9 August 1924.

The list of subjects was printed by a Welsh firm in Liverpool. It had advertisements on alternate pages, with English predominating. This again demonstrates that Welsh was still denied any commercial value. But one paper recorded that there were advertisements of the Eisteddfod in

London and other English newspapers — some of them 'almost doing justice to Welsh'!

The fourteen committees show the immense interest of the inhabitants of Pontypool and its environs in their Eisteddfod long before it took place. By July 1923, the official booklet with the list of subjects for competition had to be completed for publication together with rules, regulations, and the amount of each prize, etc. It meant that all the committees involved had to meet regularly and the secretaries had to keep stringently correct minutes as well as correspond with many people. In addition to this, the official programme for each day of the Eisteddfod needed to be worked out, presidents to be secured, timing and location of preliminary tests as well as events in the pavilion to be arranged so that clashes might be avoided, as well as a host of other arrangements to be made so that the Eisteddfod could run smoothly.

The success of the Pontypool Eisteddfod again meant close co-operation, loyalty, devotion, effort and faith for the sake of the Welsh language and the Welsh tradition in Gwent. It is quite extraordinary that such a gargantuan task could be completed in time; but that is what happened, and it is interesting to note that the programmes contained more Welsh than the 1913 Eisteddfod in Abergavenny.

The subjects chosen for the special prizes were, for example, 'The Pioneers of the Welsh Coalfield' and 'A Monmouthshire Bibliography'. There was a wide variety in the literature section for adults and school children. Welsh had become more evident in the music competitions, one of them being the composition of a tone poem for full orchestra based on Branwen, from the *Mabinogi*. Schools were catered for to a greater extent and use was made of a number of Welsh books and oral work. In the programme the Arts, Crafts and Science section was in English except for slate-splitting, and line drawing depicting incidents in a choice of one of three Welsh books. A greater effort was made to draw non-Welsh speakers to compete.

The official programme was full of advertisements, with the majority yet again in English. The names of guarantors and members of the general committee filled eleven pages, and the names of those on the different committees with photographs of the most important officials covered thirty-six. All except two advertisements of society meetings were in Welsh. One advertisement was particularly interesting: a Welsh Holiday School in Llanwrtyd on 11 and 12 August where there would be classes in Welsh — one being on Welsh teaching methods in schools. There were special Welsh classes for English speakers and for Sunday School work. The Gorsedd ceremonies took place on Pen-y-garn Hill on two mornings, and, as one would expect, were in Welsh only. The ceremonies were under the jurisdiction of the Archdruid, Elfed, minister of Kings Cross Congregational Church, London, a poet and hymn-writer.

There was a special tent for the literary section of the Eisteddfod, an innovation which proved most successful. Drama found another stage outside the pavilion, but the chairing and crowning ceremonies were still held there. The pavilion, which could accommodate at least 15,000, was opened on Monday morning by the Rt. Hon. Thomas Richards, secretary of the South Wales Miners' Federation. Everyone could see the platform clearly and amplifiers carried his voice to the farthest corners, so that every word of the speaker's patriotic speech was audible. The walls were adorned with the names of departed poets and other Welsh celebrities. He was heard to say that Gwent was as Welsh in spirit as any part of Wales and that in the Eisteddfod there was an elimination of class and creed. Wales could lead the world in the direction of peace, but the Welsh needed to develop and cultivate confidence, aggressiveness and assertiveness. The Archdruid spoke in Welsh as well as in English, telling his audience that Wales could build a Temple of Peace which would inspire the nations.

The evening concert was given by children from nine schools who sang in both English and Welsh, including a Welsh version of the Londonderry Air! The *penillion* singing was of course in Welsh, the concert ending with the Welsh National Anthem. Tuesday saw a crowded pavilion to welcome the Prince of Wales. He came on stage, was invested and robed appropriately, befitting his status in the Gorsedd;

The Gorsedd circle at Pontypool, 1924.
(*By permission of Torfaen Museum Trust.*)

Archdruid Elfed with Prosser Rhys (the crowned bard) and
Prince Edward at the 1924 National Eisteddfod.
(*By permission of Mr. Rhisiart Hincks.*)

the Archdruid greeted him in Welsh, he made a short reply, and left to deafening applause inside and outside the pavilion. The same day saw the ceremony of the crowning of the bard for a poem on one of the following subjects: 'Atgof' ('Recollection'), 'Dafydd ap Gwilym' and 'Marchog yr Awyr' ('The Knight of the Air'), the prize being £20 as well as a crown. The adjudicators, also three poets, W.J. Gruffydd (Professor of Welsh at the University College of South Wales and Monmouthshire, as it was then called), Crwys (a Welsh Congregational minister) and Gwili (a Welsh Baptist minister), proclaimed it the worst competition for many years with the exception of the poem written by 'Daedalus'. Gruffydd forecast that there would be much argument about its contents for many years, for 'Daedalus' had written a challenging poem of literary value. Indeed, his *pryddest* was a masterpiece compared with the *pryddestau* which had been crowned in previous years. It was revealed that the poet was a 23-year-old journalist from Aberystwyth, Prosser Rhys. He published no poetry after 1924; yet, as editor of *Baner ac Amserau Cymru*, he did much to encourage young aspiring poets and writers.

A minister and twice-crowned bard from north Wales, Albert Evan-Jones, (Cynan) won the chair, for his *awdl* 'I'r Duw nid Adweinir' ('To the Unknown God'). The craftsmanship in his poem made it the best of the twelve submitted. He was a master of the Welsh language and of Welsh poetry in the strict metres. It was he who fashioned the *Dawns Flodau* (Flower Dance) for the Gorsedd, the crowning and chairing ceremonies. As an actor and playwright he contributed much to the Welsh theatre.

A much-loved poet, Eifion Wyn (Eliseus Williams) of Porthmadog won several prizes for lyrics in strict and free verse, among them was his lyric poem 'Cwm Pennant', for which he became known and loved by Welsh people the world over.

The chief choral competition was the main attraction to the huge gathering in the pavilion and on the Eisteddfod field on the Wednesday. A great commotion occurred when a 'foreign' choir won and not a choir from Gwent, which was the favourite of the audience.

There was an opinion gathering strength that the Eisteddfod was increasingly serving music rather than poetry. Saunders Lewis, in his address to the University Union, emphasized the pressing need for all those concerned to be aware of this. On a similar theme, the Archdruid appealed to all the bards to realize that they were going through a period of change in poetry. If only the young poets would be more courteous and the older poets more broadminded, he saw no obstacle to understanding and co-operation between them all.

During the Eisteddfod some of the societies held memorable meetings. The Honourable Society of Cymmrodorion met, with Lord Treowen presiding, to discuss art and architecture in Wales: Lord Treowen felt that there would be no art unless there was harmony between words and music and between paintings and the buildings which housed them. He wanted to see a National School of Art in Wales and Goscombe John, in a letter to Vincent Evans (which was read out), wanted art to be on every school curriculum. Clough Williams-Ellis, of Portmeirion fame, and T. Alwyn Lloyd (architect and town planner), praised Cardiff's superb civic centre, the National Library of Wales, Aberystwyth, and the University College of North Wales, Bangor, as notable examples of modern public buildings.

The status of Welsh drama, however, was a source of concern; it needed a new impetus. Robert Atkins (Director of Productions at the Old Vic) suggested that a central bureau be established to register all the Welsh dramatic companies. A catalogue of plays could be made to form a drama library where work by Welsh authors should be given preference. Yet he also urged the Welsh drama movement to keep in touch with other movements world wide. Another suggestion was that the form of the pageant should be encouraged and developed to enable as many members of the community as possible to participate. The Welsh playwright, J.O. Francis, declared that the bane of the drama movement at that time was the casual and easy-going nature of Welsh play production. He proposed a Welsh summer school to instruct play producers.

Once again during this Eisteddfod, as in 1913 at Aber-gavenny, Lloyd George failed to appear for his presidential address due to pressure of work before the parliamentary summer recess. However, it was noted that the following day he did go to Carmarthen to support Alfred Mond as Liberal candidate in the local by-election! Ramsay MacDonald, the Prime Minister, also failed to appear, pleading pressure of work. The historian, Joseph Bradney, however, delivered a rousing speech. He declared that the Eisteddfod had been most successful in spite of doubts that Pontypool was neither sufficiently Welsh nor had enough patriotic enthusiasm to hold the event. All those doubts had been proved wrong. Throughout the years, through the Eisteddfod, ideas had flowed which would improve Wales in many ways. Thus Wales had established its own University, National Library and National Museum. He was proud and gratified that Wales had such foundations of its own instead of being a 'hanger-on' and a humble participator in similar foundations in England.

Once more a National Eisteddfod in Gwent had proved its worth. Its activities had reverberated throughout Wales, confirming the Welsh tradition, not only of Pontypool, but of the whole of Gwent.

The 1958 Eisteddfod

The National Eisteddfod of Glynebwy (Ebbw Vale) from 4 to 9 August 1958, proved to be a success in spite of inclement weather. According to the *Western Mail* it was friendly and cosmopolitan and full of surprises. By that year a 'Welsh rule' had been established, which meant that everything should be conducted through the medium of Welsh. Sadly, deviations from that rule occurred. For instance Aneurin Bevan (the local Welsh MP from 1929 to 1960) came as one of the presidents and delivered his address in English. His parents, though they were Welsh speaking and had given their children resounding Welsh names, like many parents in other parts of Wales, had not transmitted the Welsh language to them. However, in his speech Bevan called the Eisteddfod a 'monument of civilization' and hoped that people would give up talking about 'Wales and Monmouthshire' for the characteristics of the people of Monmouthshire were Welsh, and, by coming to Monmouthshire, the Eisteddfod united the county with the rest of Wales.

On 31 July a young man from Cardiff, E.G. Millward, wrote an article for *Baner ac Amserau Cymru*. He had learned Welsh in Cathays High School for Boys and had proceeded to the University College, Cardiff, had studied Welsh there, mastered the language thoroughly and gained a first class degree. He deplored the fact that the Glynebwy Eisteddfod had opened the door to English by even a chink. The *Western Mail* had been calling for less Welsh at the Eisteddfod for the sake of the non-Welsh-speakers, but Millward pointed out that the most intelligent non-Welsh-speakers had already seen the value of the Eisteddfod as a Welsh institution. He mentioned two MPs (not from Monmouthshire) who were in the forefront of the battle against its Welshness and who cared not an iota about the Welsh language and things Welsh. He went on to say that the Eisteddfod was not meant to be a 'popular' institution but one through which the Welsh people could express what was best in their culture. Furthermore, the Eisteddfod took up *only* one week of a whole year, and in that one week all parts of Wales were united.

The Welsh people who were deeply interested in the Eisteddfod and who were regular attenders wherever it was held in Wales were not slow to see that much of it called for improvement. They alone were its rightful critics and they minced no words. To them the Eisteddfod was not a static institution but had to move forward, keeping a wary eye on things Welsh, especially the preservation of the language. The week before the Eisteddfod several articles appeared in *Baner ac Amserau Cymru* doing just that. R. Gerallt Jones criticized adjudications for their poor standard and frequent dependence on personal taste. Kate Roberts criticized the Eisteddfod for its lack of consideration of the novel, and the prose medal ceremony for its lack of dignity. Selwyn Jones praised the success of the Youth Orchestra of Wales, which started its life in Gwent, and the scores of teachers who had taught the children to pronounce the Welsh words they were to sing. He drew the attention of the Monmouthshire County Council to this fact and hoped that its members would realize that the success of the Eisteddfod would be due to hard work by volunteers in Gwent itself. Another article, by George Davies, declared that a *theatr fach* (a little theatre) on the Eisteddfod field was essential. A *theatr fach* would be a meeting place where actors and playwrights could discuss their craft, and would add to the already significant contribution made by the Eisteddfod to the improvement in the standard of Welsh play-writing during the previous half century.

The fact that English was allowed on the pavilion platform gave rise to the fear that the Eisteddfod would again revert to being bilingual. The secretaries of the Eisteddfod Court, however, emphasized in their annual report that there would be no relaxation of the Welsh rule in future — and there never has been. The Welsh rule in Glynebwy had meant that hundreds of the inhabitants of the county had become interested in learning Welsh. The local press had for months been printing sentences in Welsh which would help them to understand the proceedings. Welsh learners were not forgotten in the competitions, nor were the children. Recognition was also given to the dialect of the area and the *Cymreigyddion y Fenni* gave a prize for a collection of records in the Gwent dialect.

The literary committee could be complimented on its *Pabell Lên* (Literature Tent), a fine and comfortable wooden structure. A number of pictures lent by the Arts Council adorned the walls. Here were heard the adjudications of all the literary competitions (except the Crown and Chair poems), and it was here too that the prizes were presented to the winners. An innovation in the *Pabell Lên* was *Senedd yr Ifanc* (Young People's Senate), where six young people commented on what kind of Welsh literature they would like in the next thirty years. Thursday afternoon saw a lively debate on the subject 'It is not the artist but the nation that creates literature'. Vincent Phillips gave a most stimulating talk on Welsh dialects, in which the audience participated. Tribute was paid to the memory and work of R. Williams

Parry, the distinguished poet, and to Rhys Bowen of Rhymni, the popular and hard-working Congregational minister there for twenty-three years. By 1958, elocution had become a fine art, and items of poetry and prose were chosen with discretion; so there was a session to discuss 'Elocution Yesterday and Today'. The *Pabell Lên* committee had to be congratulated for its inspiration to extend and revise its activities — the only complaint being that there were so many of them and so little time to do them justice.

Sir Daniel T. Davies, the royal physician, emphasized the Welshness of Gwent. Citing Arthur Machen and W.H. Davies, he commented that, though they wrote poetry in English, the warmth of the Celt was in their work. He mentioned Islwyn and Tre-fin as examples of 'the honourable roll of Welsh poets'. Like other speakers, he wondered when the world would recognize the contribution to peace that Wales had made over the centuries. Saunders Lewis, one of the outstanding Welsh men of letters and a political and cultural force, was one of the Eisteddfod presidents and delivered a patriotic speech appealing to his audience to defend the land of Wales more courageously. He began by referring to the government's determination to examine the location near Trawsfynydd in order to build a nuclear power station and went on to describe the slogans carried at a demonstration by those who were in favour of the station — 'Bread before beauty' and 'Pylons before poverty'. Our forefathers, he declared, knew of much better ones — *Gwell angau na chywilydd* (Better death than dishonour) and *Gwell tlodi na gwarth* (Better poverty than disgrace). He and those listening to him, he continued, had no right to the land of Wales, as it was theirs for but a short time and really belonged to their children and their children's children for generations to come. He implored all Welsh people to respect and to defend their children's heritage, not to sell it for a 'mess of pottage', and not to barter priceless Welsh assets 'for the mirage of materialistic progress'. How relevant his message still is in the latter half of the twentieth century — and how prophetic.

The Bishop of Bangor (later Archbishop of Wales), the Rt. Revd G.O. Williams, deplored the idea that Wales might lose

Jennie Lee, Aneurin Bevan and Paul Robeson in the audience of the National Eisteddfod at Ebbw Vale, 1958.
(By permission of the National Eisteddfod of Wales.)

her language. The Eisteddfod was one institution through which the Welsh could defend and strengthen it. He declared that God's judgement fell upon those who ignored it for the sake of material success. It was only by being faithful to themselves that the Welsh could contribute to the good and peace of the world.

Sam Jones, Head of the BBC in Bangor, who had just completed a quarter of a century serving radio in Wales, declared in his presidential address that it should be made known that there was but one Welsh nation, not a nation divided into North and South. He felt he had a right to say this for he knew Welsh people all over Wales. *Urdd Gobaith Cymru* (the Wales League of Youth) had brought together children and young people from all parts of Wales and the Eisteddfod had brought their parents. Radio had made dialects intelligible to all. Television was on the way. Welsh people should grasp the opportunity it would give, to make sure it would be for the good of Wales and the Welsh language. He envisaged that Wales would ask for its own television station, so it was necessary to decide in time how best it could be secured. In those days, Welsh programmes were televised only at times when there was no call for English ones!

As usual there were ceremonies for crowning and chairing during the Eisteddfod. The subject of the *pryddest* for the crown was 'Cymod' ('Reconciliation') which, according to the three adjudicators, was a disappointing competition, though sixteen long poems were submitted. The subject of the *awdl*, for the chair, was 'Caerllion-ar-Wysg' ('Caerleon-upon-Usk') and only six had competed. The fact that both crowned and chaired bards had similar names and came from the same county, Ceredigion (Cardiganshire), created some confusion. The former was Llewelyn Jones of Llanbadarn, who was on the staff of the National Library. The latter was T. Llew Jones, a productive poet and author of books for young people which filled a gap in their literature for a long while. In his poem he depicts a grandfather seeing his grandson fraternizing with the Romans in Caerleon, learning their language and their ways, and as a result turning his back upon Wales and the Welsh language. It is sad to say that this theme is as relevant today as is Saunders Lewis's message.

The Sunday saw a *Cymanfa Ganu* (Hymn Singing Festival) in the pavilion, and the visit of Paul Robeson, the famous Negro singer, who was presented with a Welsh hymn-book to mark the occasion.

A different play was acted each night, some of which were translations into Welsh. Saunders Lewis had been commissioned for the Eisteddfod and presented his play *Brad* ('Treason'). Based on the unsuccessful plot to assassinate Hitler in July 1944 by the military hierarchy in Germany, the play was a resounding success. The playwrights John Gwilym Jones and John Ellis Williams held an enlightened and detailed discussion about this play in *Y Babell Lên*; *Brad* has been acted many times since on Welsh television and translated into English and German. There were translations of *Hamlet*, *Juno and the Paycock* and Anouilh's *Antigone*. Other plays written in Welsh included *Glo i'r Marwor* ('Coal to the Embers') by Gwynne D. Evans and *Y Ferch a'r Dewin* ('The Maiden and the Magician') by F.G. Fisher (a native of Bargoed). Play-acting competitions were also held for full-length and one-act plays.

Eight national societies held meetings at the Eisteddfod. One public meeting was held to celebrate the centenary of the author, litterateur, historian, educationist and editor, Sir Owen M. Edwards, and his son, Sir Ifan ab Owen Edwards, founder of Urdd Gobaith Cymru, chaired the meeting of *Undeb y Cymry ar Wasgar* (Union of Welsh People outside Wales).

Musical concerts were presented every night with fully bilingual programmes, including details of the concert and the composers. The Gwent String Orchestra played for the children, who sang in Welsh in a choir drawn from forty-one Gwent schools. No Welsh was taught in those schools; so those who taught the children to sing had to teach them how to pronounce the words also. Mozart's *Requiem* was sung in Latin. On Wednesday the National Youth Orchestra performed to the delight of all and on the last night the Welsh National Opera sang Verdi's *I Lombardi*. Great anxiety was felt that there were not enough pieces with Welsh words set to music — both traditional and modern. There was a call for co-operation between the University of Wales Press and the Music Council so as not to lose the opportunity given by the 'Welsh rule.'

The courage of the people of Glynebwy to face the challenge of holding an Eisteddfod was praiseworthy, to say the least. But, as Tre-fin wrote in an article in a Welsh paper, the descendants of the Welsh-speaking Welsh in Gwent who had lost so much of the language had worked as energetically and as fervently as those Welsh speakers who had just come to the county to live. The attendance at the Eisteddfod was so high that an overflow pavilion had to be added.

Each Eisteddfod in Gwent had re-awakened the national consciousness of the Welsh people of Gwent and of the rest of Wales. Grateful thanks must go to those gallant and optimistic people who ventured to hold the Eisteddfod four times, between 1897 and 1958, thus helping to continue the tradition of the Welsh national cultural institution. Those closely involved in all four rose to the occasion. Indeed, the Eisteddfodau in Newport, Abergavenny, Pontypool and Ebbw Vale each contributed something special, though many feared that there might not be the necessary support in Gwent. Those fears were unfounded. Thus Gwent has indeed played its part like any other county in Wales in the history of the National Eisteddfod, and by so doing, it has also helped to preserve the Welsh literary tradition in Gwent itself. As Professor Griffith John Williams explained in his lecture to the Union of Welsh Teachers in the *Pabell Lên* in Ebbw Vale, Gwent has most certainly always been part of Wales.

3

Printers, Publishers and Authors

M ANY printers and publishers of Gwent have been very aware of the county's Welsh identity. One of these was John Edward Southall (1855–1928), printer, publisher, author and a native of Leominster, a committed Quaker who wrote many books about his faith. He had learned Welsh as a young man before coming to Newport in 1879 and establishing himself as a printer. During the following forty years he also worked as a publisher and a writer and was extremely conscious of the Welsh language and the way it was taught to both Welsh speaking and non-Welsh speaking children. He gave evidence before the Royal Commission on Education (1886–87) on 'Bilingual teaching in Welsh elementary schools'. The Welsh Language Census of 1891 provoked him to write a booklet in 1895 including a section with 'Remarks on the future of the language'. He was deeply concerned about Welsh and had already, in 1892, written *Wales and her language considered from a historical, educational and social standpoint* (second edition 1893), and a host of other books followed in swift succession, making him one of the leading publishers of Welsh and bilingual books for schools. The touching choice he made for his bardic name was 'Galar Gwent' (The Grief of Gwent). His books to help school children learn the language were of great assistance in the Gwent eisteddfodau of the early twentieth century. He was also a member of the first *Cymdeithas yr Iaith Gymraeg* (Welsh Language Society), founded in 1885.

Another author who lived during the same period was the historian and bibliographer, William Haines of Penpergwm, a collector of many books, manuscripts, documents and photographs relating to Gwent. After his death in 1922, Sir

Garrod Thomas and his wife bought most of his collection and two years later presented it to the Newport library. Haines also assembled a bibliography of the county, an immense work which entailed minute care, and now housed at the National Library, Aberystwyth, in ten unpublished manuscript volumes.

The first printing press in Gwent was established by a Welsh Baptist minister, Miles Harry, born in Bedwellty in 1700 to a family of well-to-do farmers. He was ordained to the ministry and, in 1731, became the first minister of a Welsh Baptist church, established primarily by himself at Pen-y-garn, near Pontypool. Ifano Jones, an authority on the history of printing in Wales, described him as an exceptional person with a strong personality, a keen intellect and tireless vitality. His influence as a preacher was great. One of the founders of the Baptist Academy in Trosnant, Pontypool, he became its first principal. Harry brought the printing press of Samuel and Felix Varley of Bristol to Gwent but it only lasted two years and closed in 1742.

For the next eighty-four years, Pontypool had no printing press, but in 1827 Richard Jones (Dolgellau) set up and managed the first of three branch printing offices in the town. Jones was the first to print *Yr Eurgrawn Wesleyaidd* ('The Wesleyan Magazine'), a periodical started in 1809. He had also printed other Welsh periodicals and had published much larger works including William Morgan's Bible in 1821. However, the output of his Pontypool press was slight and his importance as a printer and publisher is based on the output of his other presses.

Richard Jones's Pontypool press was bought in 1829 by William Rowlands, a native of Tregaron, who, though he knew nothing about the business of printing, was an author and publisher as well as a minister with the Calvinistic Methodists. As soon as he bought the press, he set about editing and publishing *Yr Athraw* ('The Teacher'), a monthly magazine for use in Sunday Schools, the last number of which appeared in 1830. By 1836 he had lost all his money, sold the business and emigrated to the United States where he went on to publish most of his Welsh output.

The first press to be established in Newport was founded in 1810 by Evan Lewis, who printed a booklet of hymns, *Caniadau'r Saint* ('Songs of the Saints') by William Roberts of Newport, another booklet of hymns in 1814, and, in 1815, a ballad, *Hanes yr hen Ŵr o'r Coed* ('The Story of the Old Man of the Woods') by Owen Evans, Newport. Lewis died suddenly in 1819.

Another printing press in High Street, Newport, owned by Samuel Etheridge, a master printer, published a booklet of new hymns, *Llef Soniarus ym Mhyrth Merch Sion* ('A Melodious Voice in the Gates of the Daughter of Zion') in 1812. The same press later printed the works of the Chartist John Frost who took it over in 1831.

Forty years later, in 1852, John C. Patterson published the first number of *The Star of Gwent*, or, to give it its longer and formal name, *The Monmouth, Glamorgan and Brecon Herald*, a paper which often manifested an interest in the Welsh literary tradition in Gwent.

On St David's Day 1867, again in Newport, a printing press owned by Thomas Williams issued the first number of a Welsh weekly called *Y Glorian* ('The Balance'). It was 'one of the best Welsh papers ever published', according to Ifano Jones. Jones also states that Thomas Williams engaged three eminent Welsh poets as editors — Islwyn, Llew Llwyfo (Lewis William Lewis, a journalist and poet who had lived in Aberdare) and Glasynys (Owen Wynne Jones, who was a curate at Pontlotyn in 1866 and then moved to Newport). Their connection with *Y Glorian* cannot be completely verified; but it is certain that, even if the three did work on *Y Glorian*, it was not for long, as the paper came to an end in July the same year. However, Thomas Williams continued to issue *The Star of Gwent* which he had acquired and which became *The Star of Gwent and South Wales Times*. Many books and pamphlets bear Thomas Williams's imprint. In 1861 Henry Evans (a former reporter on *The Star of Gwent*) printed the first volume of the second series of *Y Bedyddiwr* (The Baptist), describing his office as 'Swyddfa y Bedyddwyr a'r *Star of Gwent*' (The Office of the Baptists and *The Star of Gwent*).

Another prominent editor and publisher mentioned by Ifano Jones arrived in Hengoed in 1809 as pastor of the Welsh Baptist Church in the parish of Gelligaer. His name was John Jenkins (alias Shôn Shincyn), a divine, an editor and a publisher, and a native of the parish of Llangynidr, Breconshire. Deprived of an education by poverty, he learned to read Welsh from a book by Morgan John Rhys, minister of Pen-y-garn Baptist Church. After settling down in Hengoed he began writing books and decided to become a master printer in order to print his Welsh commentary on every verse in the Bible. He built a shed in Maes-y-Cwmmwr to house the press and called it *Argraffdy'r Beirdd* ('The Poets' Printing Press'). After moving it for a short while to Merthyr Tudful, he returned in 1827 to Maes-y-Cwmmwr, where he built a house and an office and continued working on his commentary. In the same year he issued the first six numbers of *Cyfrinach y Bedyddwyr* ('The Secret of the Baptists'), a monthly of which he was editor and largest contributor. Together with his sons, he went on to publish other Baptist magazines (while editing some of them himself).

Jenkins's works also include a collection of hymns and a series of booklets for Sunday Schools. He was a man 'of industry and perseverance in the face of extraordinary obstacles', according to Ifano Jones, who added: 'his work is extremely good'. His printing press was one of the largest in Wales at the time, and his son Llewelyn continued the family tradition, becoming a benefactor of the Welsh press, an editor, author and publisher. In 1859, six years after the death of his father, Llewelyn collaborated with his brother John, to write John Jenkins's biography.

In Tredegar, in 1859, William Harris (brother of Joseph Harris, Gomer) printed his *Athrawydd: sef Hyfforddydd i Ddarllen*, a reading manual. He was also the first in Gwent to publish a newspaper for the valleys which he called *The Tredegar Iron Times* and which was printed by Charles Peaty.

At one time, in Gelli-groes, the poet Aneurin Jones (Aneurin Fardd) owned a printing press, and had ambitious intentions, enlarging his office in order to accommodate *Y Bedyddiwr*; he also intended to print many Welsh books, including a history of the Baptists. However, his period as a printer lasted only two and a half years, till 1864; thus his production was confined to a number of booklets. Although a company had been formed in 1859 with Aneurin Jones as business manager and Thomas Williams of *The Star of Gwent* as printer, the venture had proved a failure. Aneurin Jones is better known for his poetry in the strict metres, as an organizer of eisteddfodau in Gelli-groes, and as an eisteddfod adjudicator, and is the subject of a Welsh lecture by the poet Tre-fin.

John Davies of Brynmawr had an office in Ebbw Vale at 51 Victoria Road — the Albion office — which printed and published the monthly periodical *Yr Ymgeisydd* ('The Candidate'), first dated 1861. It was acquired by him for the use of the Calvinistic Methodists in south Wales, with Islwyn and Dewi Wyn o Essyllt (Thomas Essile Davies) as editors; but it was wound up in 1862.

Joseph Alfred Bradney, born in Shropshire and educated at Harrow and Cambridge, served Wales in many spheres — as a prominent member of the councils of the National Library, the National Museum and Monmouthshire county. But it is as the historian of his adopted county that he is best known. The first volume of his *History of Monmouthshire* was published in 1904, and part of the fourth in 1932, but he did not live to complete the latter. It was Bradney who published *Hanes Llanffwyst* by Evan Watkins (Eiddil Ifor) in 1922 which was printed by the Minerva Press, Abergavenny. The list of Bradney's own works is a lengthy one, including in 1926 the publication of his *A Memorandum, being an attempt to give a chronology of the Welsh language in the Eastern part of the County of Monmouth.* He copied and published several parish registers. For his services to his county and for his scholarship, he received many honours, among them the honorary degree of D.Litt. of the University of Wales. Had he produced nothing other than his *History of Monmouth-shire*, Gwent would be eternally grateful to him as one of its best adopted sons. Even though he wrote in English, he could speak Welsh, and his awareness of Welsh is evident in all his works. He was a member of the Gorsedd with the bardic name 'Achydd Glan Troddi' (The Genealogist of Glan Troddi).

Antiquary, historian and litterateur, William Roberts (Nefydd), came to Gwent as Baptist minister of Salem, Blaenau Gwent, in 1845, living there till his death in 1872. He bought Aneurin Jones's press in 1864 in order to print the history of the Baptists, which had long before been a dream of his. As an essayist, competing and adjudicating in the eisteddfodau of the day were additional interests. For four years prior to his death he printed and published *Y Bedyddiwr*; he also edited *Seren Gomer* but printed only one number of it. In addition, he established and examined schools and organized the training of teachers. His library numbered some 6,000 printed books as well as manuscripts. Among the latter are the diaries of Edmund Jones and other manuscripts he had collected together with his own manuscripts and letters, (which are now housed in the National Library). Ifano Jones says of him that,

> his articles in the *Encyclopaedia Cambrensis* (1856–79) and in Welsh periodicals are splendid evidence of his all-round equipment as a scientific historian, and are the basis and inspiration of very much of recently written work on religious and educational movements in Wales from the sixteenth century to the eighteenth.

One of Gwent's famous musical sons was William Aubrey Williams (Gwilym Gwent). Born in Tredegar in 1838, he was the most popular Welsh composer during his lifetime and also assisted in editing *Llwybrau Moliant* ('Paths of Praise') for the Welsh Baptists.

In 1870, John Davies, a man of many talents, was appointed minister of the Calvinistic Methodist churches of Pandy and Forest Pit, near Abergavenny. In addition to writing innumerable articles for the Welsh and English press, and helping Joseph Bradney to gather material for his *History of Monmouthshire*, he was a Fellow of the Society of Antiquaries, an alderman of the county council, chairman of his parish council, and a Justice of the Peace. One of the greatest influences on his work was Thomas Stephens, author of *The Literature of the Kymry*.

No account of the Welsh cultural tradition of Gwent should omit mentioning Edmund Jones, of Pontypool, a Congregational minister, author, and son of Gwent, born in the parish of Aberystruth. Jones published a book of sermons but is best remembered for his *Historical Account of the Parish of Aberystruth* (1779) which contains many important facts, and also for his collection of folk legends, *A Relation of Apparitions in the Principality of Wales* (1780). He used to prophesy, and several of his prophecies turned out to be true. For that reason he was given the pseudonym 'Yr Hen Broffwyd' (The Old Prophet). His diaries in the National Library are full of news about religious developments and were saved just in time before being used by a Pontypool shopkeeper to pack his wares . . .

In 1849 a book was published in London with the title, *Wales, the Language, Social Condition, Moral Character, and Religious Opinions of the People considered in their relation to Education* by Sir Thomas Phillips. It is an important work, for it discusses one of the most traumatic events in the history of the Welsh language. Two years before it was published, there appeared in three volumes, with blue covers, reports published by the government of the time on the state of education in Wales, the result of a Royal Commission 'to enquire into the means afforded the labouring classes of acquiring a knowledge of the English language'. Three Commissioners were appointed to consider, after they had studied the situation, what should be done to improve 'the existing means of education in Wales'. The three were Englishmen with no knowledge of the Welsh language (which they called 'a peculiar language'). Neither could they understand a word of what was being said to them by monoglot Welsh adults and children whom they met or interviewed; nor did they, as a result, show them any sympathy or patience. Instead, they accepted the word of those who were themselves hostile to the Welsh language and wished to get rid of it. Sadly, many of those people were clerics of the Established Church who would testify against the Dissenters whenever they had a chance — and the Dissenters were Welsh speaking. Thomas Phillips was a successful barrister and also a member of the Established Church, but he saw the gross unfairness of the reports of the Commissioners, including Symons, who was the one who came to Gwent. In his book, Phillips treats Symons's 'evidence' as 'erroneous statements and unsound conclusions'. He goes as far as to say that the Commission should have been entrusted to Welshmen. His evidence methodically breaks down every statement in the reports from the standpoint of a Welshman and a barrister. He deplored their apparent vindictiveness and the way in which the Welsh people had been described in them as though they were the scum of the earth. To this day the reports of the Commission are known as *Brad y Llyfrau Gleision* ('The Treason of the Blue Books').

Sir Thomas Phillips was born in the parish of Llanelli, Breconshire, in 1801, but came with his parents to live in Trosnant, near Pontypool — at an age young enough to be considered a native of Gwent. He studied to be a lawyer in Newport and in 1838 and 1839 was mayor of the town. No doubt he knew many of the Chartists — especially John Frost. He spent many years in London as a successful barrister, but later in life he returned to Gwent to live at Llanellen near Abergavenny.

His book shows his wide knowledge of Welsh literature and history and of the growth of the Nonconformist denominations — the Dissenters — in Wales. The book is a monument to his Welshness, to his masterly indictment of the false vilification of the Welsh people by the English Commission of 1847, and to its prejudicial, defamatory and malicious reports.

In 1845 Evan Jones, or Ieuan Gwynedd, as he is known, came to Gwent from his native Sir Feirionnydd (Merionethshire) as minister of Saron, the Welsh Congregational Church in Tredegar. Because of ill-health, however, he remained there for only two years. In 1849 he became editor of *Y Gymraes* ('The Welshwoman') — the first paper of its kind for Welsh women — with Lady Llanover as its patron. It is good to record that the paper sold better in Gwent than anywhere else in Wales. Ieuan Gwynedd also wrote a biographical article about Edmund Jones in *Yr Adolygydd*

('The Reviewer') in 1850. He, too, attacked the 'findings of the Commissioners', as a Dissenter and a Welshman, and wrote many articles in English and Welsh papers, one being the *Monmouthshire Merlin*. He collected facts and figures meticulously and was as forceful in his arguments as Thomas Phillips. His *Vindication of the Educational and Moral Condition of Wales in reply to William Williams, Esq., Late MP for Coventry* was published in 1848. After his death in 1852, Lord and Lady Llanover showed his widow much kindness and engaged her to draw up an index of their large library.

Southall also refers to the work of the Commissioner and his treatment of *The Treason of the Blue Books* is as logical and reasonable as that of Thomas Phillips and Ieuan Gwynedd. In addition, he advocated the use of Welsh in the schools at the end of the nineteenth century and offered suggestions on how to implement it. Indeed, in his time, he was one of the most forceful promoters of Welsh. This work, in addition to the works of Thomas Phillips and Ieuan Gwynedd, would be a most valuable reference book for those teaching and learning about the history of Wales in the nineteenth century.

4

Poets of Gwent

IN the last quarter of the eighteenth century and the first
half of the nineteenth, the Industrial Revolution was at its
height in parts of Gwent. New ironworks were opened in
the eighteenth century at Sirhowy, Beaufort, Ebbw Vale,
Blaenafon and Nantyglo and many people left their farms,
turning their backs on agriculture to work in the new industry
and, they hoped, to earn more money. Later, works were
opened in Tredegar in the parish of Bedwellty, and as a result
the population increased from 619 in 1801 to 10,637 in 1831.
New and highly successful processes using coal were developed in Merthyr Tudful. Sirhowy possessed all that was
necessary for the new processes — iron ore, coal, lime, sand,
water . . . and a railway. So, here, were opened the first
ironworks in Gwent to use the new processes. Soon the
population increased yet again.

Among those who flocked to the Sirhowy valley were
Welsh people from Llangynidr, Merthyr Tudful, the Neath
Valley and as far afield as Cardigan, Tregaron and other small
towns and villages in west Wales. They became fitters,
puddlers, carriers, smiths, carpenters, masons, weighers,
stablemen and so on — all followed trades necessary for the
maintenance and running of the ironworks. Life was hard and
uncertain. The houses were uncomfortable, to say the least,
and unhealthy with no sanitation; the streets were unlit,
unpaved and rough.

For this deplorable state of affairs, the 1847 Commission
did not blame the ironmasters but the ordinary working folk
who toiled long hours for small wages. They were recorded in
the report of the Commission as being filthy, immoral and
unintelligent, with the whole region, except for Newport,

being a scene of filth and untidiness. They were said to be as strong as animals and completely lacking moral, mental and spiritual qualities. Yet, among those who were so maligned by the Commissioner (the Englishman Symons), dwelt a large community of Welsh people who built chapels, attended them regularly and were engaged in Welsh cultural pursuits. They were supporters of the eisteddfodau held by *Cymdeithas Cymreigyddion y Fenni* and were avid readers of the current Welsh periodicals, especially *Seren Gomer* which reported foreign and British news, fairs and markets and the movement of ships, and published letters, poetry and general articles. They brought Nonconformity with them, and in its turn that Nonconformity brought as their ministers some of the leading Welshmen of the day. The Welsh poetic tradition was an integral part of the lives of many of them.

Gwent possessed many literary characters in this period, one of whom William Williams (Myfyr Wyn), recalled the stories of some of these people in his *Atgofion am Sirhowy a'r Cylch* ('Memories of Sirhowy and District'). Eight years after his death in 1900, his brother published a collection of his works, entitled *Cân, Llên a Gwerin* ('Song, Literature and Folk') — a nostalgic account of people whom he knew when he lived in Sirhowy. A blacksmith by trade, Myfyr Wyn had also published amusing booklets of poetry and recitations and was a regular contributor to the radical paper, *Tarian y Gweithiwr* ('The Worker's Shield') — often in the Gwentian dialect.

Myfyr Wyn recalls Brychan Bach (John Davies) from north Breconshire, editor and a promoter of friendly societies. The family moved to Sirhowy after the father's death, and Davies became a foreman underground and was for four years a bookseller and publisher. Friends of his included Iolo Morganwg, Carnhuanawc and Cynddelw. His *Llais Awen Gwent a Morgannwg* ('The Voice of the Muse of Gwent and Morgannwg') appeared in 1824 followed by numerous other booklets of poetry. Like other Gwentian poets, Brychan Bach was held in high regard by Gwenynen Gwent. Myfyr Wyn also writes of Eiddil Gwent (David Morris), who spent most of his life in Tredegar as a cobbler, and, like Brychan, was a prominent member of *Cymreigyddion y Fenni*. He won a prize in the 1862 Tredegar Cymmrodorion Eisteddfod for his history of Tredegar, (later published in 1868). Another poet included was Gwentydd (Joseph Bevan) a blacksmith, remembered by Myfyr Wyn as a genial person, who was considered a learned and knowledgeable man. Gwentydd possessed a very good library (most unusual at the time) and was constantly reading. He would also hold a night school in the winter and write letters on behalf of many illiterate folk, and for twenty years distributed the paper *Seren Cymru* to which he himself contributed a great deal of prose and poetry. His ballad 'Can mlynedd i nawr' ('A hundred years from now') was popular and is still remembered.

Cadwgan, well-known amongst the poets of Wales and America, was an ordinary worker in the ironworks but was successful in many eisteddfodau. In 1849 he won a prize in *Seren Gomer* for an elegy to Carnhuanawc. The elegy and Cynddelw's ode 'Yr Atgyfodiad' ('The Resurrection') were included in *Gwentwyson*, the booklet published in 1849 by Evan Jones (Gwrwst) containing elegies in memory of Carnhuanawc. Gwrwst had been minister of Castleton Baptist Church between 1823 and 1855 when the members of his church increased and branches were opened in nearby villages.

The poet and musician Gwentwyson (Ezekiel Davies) was a blacksmith and native of Sirhowy. Gwentydd, Myfyr Wyn and he were firm friends. They would discuss poetry and the intricacies of *cynghanedd* and practise their art in chalk on the sheets of the smithy, covering them with lines of *cywyddau*.

There were others, who lived in the Twyn, to whom Myfyr Wyn refers with affection. One character, Bilo Llwyd, frequented local eisteddfodau and sang to harp accompaniment. He was considered a fine *penillion* singer. Another was William Morgan, who took his bardic name, Gwilym Gellideg, from a little village near Merthyr Tudful. He worked at one time in Rhymni and was initiated into the Gorsedd in 1837 at the Abergavenny Eisteddfod. His main interest was competing at eisteddfodau as a poet and singer; he was also known as a music adjudicator. Thousands of copies of his well-known ballad 'Ple byddaf mhen can mlynedd?' were sold in fairs and public houses. In 1846 a selection of his poetry appeared under the title, *Cerbyd Awen* ('Coach of the Muse').

In his book, Myfyr Wyn quotes from an account in *Seren Gomer* of the life of William Hopkin, his mother's brother, by the Revd Thomas Lewis. Hopkin was notable for his contribution to a Welsh *Biblical and Theological Dictionary*, the work of John Jones (Mathetes). A minister of Penuel, Rhymni and Siloam, Tafarnau Bach, Mathetes was a writer of repute. He was successful in many eisteddfodau, published scores of articles (mainly in *Seren Gomer*) and published theological books. Mathetes was also one-time co-editor of two Welsh Baptist papers.

Myfyr Wyn writes with great affection about one other person, namely Cynddelw. While minister of Carmel Baptist Church, Sirhowy, Cynddelw was left a widower with four young children to rear. He had come there as a comparatively young man in 1847, remained there for fifteen years, and certainly spent his most productive literary years in Gwent. His *awdl*, 'Yr Atgyfodiad', brought him fame in 1849. In 1853 he published *Tafol y Beirdd*, a standard work for many years on the rules of poetry in the strict metres. The greatest part of his work *Esboniad ar y Testament Newydd* ('A Commentary on the New Testament') was compiled in Sirhowy.

Thomas Twynog Jeffreys (Twynog) and John Davies (Ossian Gwent) were poets, the former the owner of a boot shop in Rhymni, the latter a pattern-maker and a carpenter in one of the Rhymni works. Jeffreys' shop was the focal point of the village literary circle. *Tannau Twynog* ('Twynog's Harp-strings') is the only small volume of his poetic work; but Dyfed (Evan Rees), Archdruid for twenty-one years, wrote an *In Memoriam* volume about him in 1911, the year of his death. Ossian Gwent's volume of *Caniadau* ('Songs') appeared in 1873 and in 1898 Southall published a volume of his hitherto unpublished works as *Blodau Gwent* ('Flowers of Gwent'). Although he moved among poets and other famous frequenters of eisteddfodau, he never competed or wrote poems in the strict metres. The two slim volumes of his works are totally different from other published poetical works of the period, for his poems are mostly about nature. Indeed it is considered that he was a greater poet than any of his contemporaries because his poetry is truly lyrical.

Aneurin Jones (Aneurin Fardd) was born in Bedwas, though his name is always connected with Gelli-groes. He received a good education, and after an apprenticeship in architecture and civil engineering pursued both professions as well as being a miller and smallholder. Aneurin Fardd became adept at writing Welsh poetry in the strict metres and, following the ancient Welsh bardic tradition, became one of Islwyn's bardic teachers. He held eisteddfodau in Gelli-groes and often adjudicated. As an adjudicator he awarded the prize to Ceiriog for his pastoral poem 'Alun Mabon' in the 1861 Aberdare Eisteddfod, and in the same year opened a printing office which he kept for two and a half years. (See Chapter 3).

John Emlyn Jones (Ioan Emlyn) was a Baptist minister. When he was only twenty years of age, he began his connection with *Cymreigyddion y Fenni*. He edited *Y Bedyddiwr* and *Seren Gomer*, but it was his poem 'Bedd y Dyn Tylawd' ('The Poor Man's Grave') which made him well-known.

Of all the poets of Gwent in the nineteenth century, the greatest and one of Wales's greatest is the Revd William Thomas (Islwyn). Tradition insists that it was Lady Llanover who suggested he adopt Islwyn as his bardic name. When he was only twenty-one years of age, he won a prize for an elegy to Carnhuanawc at the 1853 Abergavenny Eisteddfod, using Islwyn as his pseudonym.

Born in the 'Agent's House' near Ynys-ddu on the Abercarn estate, the youngest of ten children, Islwyn received his education entirely through the medium of English, in Tredegar, Newport and Cowbridge. English, it is said, was the language of his home; yet, he must have been conversant with Welsh before his brother-in-law, the Revd Daniel Jenkins, minister of Y Babell, the Methodist chapel in Ynysddu (in the shadow of whose wall the poet was later buried), took him under his wing and encouraged him to train for the

Edgar Phillips (Tre-fîn).
(By permission of the National Library of Wales.)

William Thomas (Islwyn).
(By permission of the National Library of Wales.)

Welsh ministry and to become interested in Welsh poetry. While he was preparing for the ministry in Swansea, he became betrothed to Anne Bowen, but shortly before they were to marry she died suddenly. This traumatic event in Islwyn's life had a tremendous impact on him. During the period 1854 to 1856 he poured his grief and anguish into two long Welsh poems, each of which is almost six thousand lines long and both of which he called *Y Storm*. In some aspects they differ from each other, though both reflect his thoughts about life, its trials and tribulations, and about death. He did not take charge of a church but rather immersed himself in poetry, eisteddfodau and Welsh periodicals. He produced two books of poems that were published during his lifetime, one in 1854 and the other in 1867.

Although he competed in eisteddfodau and won several chairs, he was not successful in the National eisteddfodau of the period. The people of Gwent have remembered him in their Eisteddfodau; and Islwyn Borough Council issued a commemorative stamp in 1982 to mark the 150th anniversary of his birth. W.J. Gruffydd begins his famous anthology of Welsh poetry with Islwyn's lines that open with 'Mae'r oll yn gysegredig' ('All is sacred'). Islwyn's hymn beginning with the line 'Gwêl uwchlaw cymylau amser' is a firm favourite. Gwent is justly proud of him as one of her most illustrious sons.

Another of Gwent's famous sons, Idris Davies, cannot be overlooked, even though he wrote most of his poetry in English. Born in the Rhymney Valley to Welsh-speaking parents he learned English at school. He became a collier at fourteen years of age but later turned to education, qualifying as a teacher, and started teaching in east London in 1932 where he became acquainted with a group of Welsh litterateurs who frequented the Welsh bookshop of the Griffiths Brothers near the Charing Cross Road. As a result he became an avid reader, especially of poetry, and began composing poetry in English. Obsessed with the wilderness in south Wales during the Depression between the two world wars, which is reflected in his *Gwalia Deserta* (1938), five years later he wrote *The Angry Summer* which gives an account of the General Strike of 1926. He expresses his intense sympathy with the unemployed, and also describes the traditions of the Welsh people, amongst whom he had been brought up, their love of reading and singing (usually in Welsh) and, naturally, the political implications of their economic distress.

Davies completed a third book, *Tonypandy and Other Poems*, in 1945, the culmination of ten years of work. After applying for teaching posts there many times, he at last returned to his beloved Rhymney Valley in 1949 but died four years later, just after his fourth book, *Selected Poems*, was published. His two first volumes are acknowledged as his greatest. His close friend and biographer, the Revd Islwyn Jenkins, has written a sensitive and sympathetic account of his life and poetry and has also edited his work.

Edgar Phillips was neither born nor brought up in Gwent, but it has to be recognized that he is one of Gwent's poets. Born in the seaside village in Pembrokeshire from which he took his bardic name Tre-fin, he had a difficult upbringing and almost lost his Welsh. As a young man he worked as a tailor, serving in the army during the First World War, then decided to go to college to become a teacher, entering Caerleon Training College in 1921. Two years later he became Welsh master in Pengam elementary school and in 1924 Welsh master in Pontllan-fraith Secondary School where he remained until his retirement in 1954.

In 1924 Tre-fin became a member of the Gorsedd of Bards in the Pontypool Eisteddfod and in 1933 was chaired at the Wrexham National Eisteddfod for his *awdl* 'Harlech'. He often competed in the National Eisteddfodau but never again won a chair, although he was very much at home in the strict metres which had to be used in that competition. Adjudicating at Eisteddfodau was another of his interests as well as attending them in his role as a prominent member of the Gorsedd. He became Archdruid in 1959. His only volume of poems, *Caniadau Trefin* (1950) is mostly in the strict metres; four other volumes entitled *Trysor o Gân* ('A Treasure of Song') were written for children from 1930 to 1936. Although Tre-fin loved Gwent as his adopted county, he often felt in exile there. His wife, Maxwell Fraser (an author and an authority on Lord and Lady Llanover) inspired and encouraged him to carry on composing poetry and writing books. Thanks to her influence, his biographer, the Archdruid Brinli, was able to say that, although he published only one volume of poetry, he was the most prolific poet of the twentieth century. Maxwell Fraser herself wrote many books in English about her adopted country: *In Praise of Wales* (1950), *Wales* (1952), *West of Offa's Dyke* (1958), and two further volumes after Tre-fin's death in 1962. Since 1986, a scholarship has been founded in her memory.

During the early 1900s several books appeared which showed an awareness of the folk tradition and literature of Gwent. One of these concerned a special type of carol called *cwndid*, popular in south-east Wales between the sixteenth and early eighteenth centuries. These carols were sung at religious festivals in the churches and were intended as moral instruction, and although they were of no intrinsic literary value, they are valuable social documents of the times. A collection of these *cwndidau* was edited by L.J.H. James (Hopcyn) and T.C. Evans (Cadrawd) in 1910 in a book entitled *Hen Gwndidau, carolau a chywyddau*.

In 1909 a Newport bookseller, John Kyrle Fletcher, published *The Gwentian Poems of Dafydd Benwyn*, a selection of the poetry of the Glamorgan poet of that name who flourished in the latter half of the sixteenth century. In 1910 a further selection of poems by the same poet appeared in the periodical *Cyfaill yr Aelwyd* ('The Friend of the Home'), in articles by T.C. Evans (Cadrawd). The collections are important because they contain a great deal of valuable information about the lineage of Gwent families to whom Dafydd Benwyn addressed so many of his poems.

In 1911 Thomas Matthews, a native of Llandybïe, Carmarthenshire, became Welsh and Geography master at Lewis School, Pengam. He must have been an ardent and inspired Welsh teacher for, in the short time he was at the school (he died in 1917), his boys, at his instigation, produced two books in 1911 and 1916. The first was entitled *Llên Gwerin Blaenau Gwent* ('The Folk Literature of the Upper Gwent Valleys'), the other *Dail Gwanwyn* ('Leaves of Spring'). They were an innovative venture for both master and pupils. The 1912 volume was the result of the master's effort to get the boys to write Welsh naturally without translating, and to collect their material orally from their own districts and not from material already published. In the poetry section, an attempt was made to use the Gwentian dialect. G.J. Jacobs and Company, Rhymni, printed the book and it was published by the school. By the time the second volume was published, the school had begun to hold annual eisteddfodau; so the book contained the work of the boys in those eisteddfodau as well as work which was done in the normal course of classwork and homework. It was a successful effort to arouse their interest and imagination. Mr. Matthews and his young students were widely congratulated, the former for his inspiration and the latter for their response. Most of them were under fifteen and a few under twelve. They could be justly proud of their efforts, for both books were a sell-out.

In 1985, at the Rhyl National Eisteddfod, the chaired bard was Robat Powel, a young man who was born and brought up in Ebbw Vale. It was only five years earlier that he began to learn the intricacies of *cynghanedd* and the strict Welsh metres. He was not from a Welsh-speaking family, nor had he learned Welsh in school in Gwent, but had learned it himself with the help of a few books and fellow-students in the University of London. He asserts that *cynghanedd* is wonderful and of course unique to Welsh, and has shattered the common belief that the use of *cynghanedd* is confined to those who come from districts in Wales which are the most strongly Welsh speaking.

5

Today and Tomorrow

A UGUST 1988 marks the return of the National Eisteddfod to Gwent, on a much larger scale than the four previous Gwent Eisteddfodau. The 1988 Eisteddfod was proclaimed in June 1987 and, according to custom, the first copy of the book containing the list of competition subjects was presented to the Archdruid at the proclamation ceremony, attended by local dignitaries as well as the Gorsedd of Bards and a large spectator public.

Welsh-speakers and non-Welsh-speakers are catered for in these competitions, and also, of course, a host of *dysgwyr* ('learners'). In addition, for those who do not understand Welsh and wish to know what is happening, technology has come to the rescue. A small, light earphone can be carried everywhere on the field offering a simultaneous translation of what is happening. Help is also freely given by the Welsh-speaking public and in the large, prominently marked tent of the *Dysgwyr*, where a full programme of Welsh-language activities is organized.

Welsh has now long been the official language of the Eisteddfod, and the 'Welsh rule' is firm and compelling. On the field, Welsh societies and organizations of all kinds have their tents, and each uses Welsh to promote its services.

The 1988 Eisteddfod offered a great variety in the subjects for competition — Welsh literature (prose and poetry), drama, elocution, music (including *cerdd dant*) and dancing. Some competitions, both written and oral, are restricted to learners. It has become the custom for some years to award a medal in a ceremony on the pavilion stage to the best *dysgwr* over twenty-one years of age who could not hold a conversation in Welsh at any level three years previously. In addition, there are art and craft, architecture, photography, ambulance and life-saving competitions in which non-Welsh-speakers may compete. Prizes are, naturally, more substantial than in previous Eisteddfodau in Gwent, while many are donated by individuals and some are sponsored by industrial and commercial bodies — a sure sign that the world of business is beginning to acknowledge that the Welsh language does have a commercial value. Special opportunities are presented to young people, and they are encouraged to sit examinations in Welsh literature and music. These examinations invariably produce work of a high standard, with a special certificate as the award and the right to become members of the Gorsedd of Bards in all its ceremonies.

The book containing the *List of Subjects* for 1988 opens with a 'Cywydd Croeso i Gasnewydd' by T.J. Harris of Rhymni. The *cywydd* is one of the ancient Welsh poetry metres that go back to the fourteenth century or earlier. T.J. Harris was a student at Caerleon College in the late 1920s. His poetry in another ancient metre — the *englyn* — which is even older (twelfth century), has won him many awards at previous eisteddfodau. Indeed, Caerleon College has played a major part in producing students and lecturers who have enriched Welsh literature, in both poetry and prose, as one of the articles at the beginning of the book states. Two articles in Welsh, one by a *dyn dwad* (an immigrant into the area), the other by a native of Gwent, give different aspects of the Welsh cultural tradition of the county.

The objects of the Eisteddfod are clear: promoting Welsh culture and safeguarding the Welsh language. It endeavours to achieve both — and succeeds. Its programme for the eight days is full of exciting activities for the young and the not so young, during the day and in the evenings. Plays and some concerts, and preliminary tests for a host of competitions have to go outside the field to find room, as do societies and movements relating to Wales and the Welsh language. The children's pageant and the concerts given by the Welsh Youth Orchestra and the Eisteddfod Choir will be in the pavilion. Time allocated for activities at *Y Babell Lên* is still too short, for the venue is always fully occupied for a variety

65

of meetings and discussions and for adjudications of the literary competitions. It is a place where poets representing a certain county compete against those of another county, and where lectures of note can be heard and members of the audience can air their views. The well-established *Theatr Fach*, where productions are presented for young and old is still too small to cope with potential audiences.

The Welsh language has made leaps and bounds in some parts of Gwent during the last fifteen or twenty years. According to the 1981 Census, it was the only county in Wales to record an increase in its Welsh speakers since the previous one. That has given an impetus to the language to increase from one to three per cent of the population, in spite of the fact that the Welsh chapels have declined. Those that remain hold one service on Sunday or share their building with an English congregation. St Woolos Cathedral honours St David with a Welsh service on the Sunday before St David's Day, and the little chapel at Llanfaches opens its doors to Welsh once or twice a year. It is not so long ago that eisteddfodau which drew large crowds were held at Mynydd Seion Welsh Congregational Chapel, Newport.

In 1961 a group of dedicated women began to hold a Welsh school on Saturday mornings for children up to thirteen years of age in a chapel vestry in Newport. In a few months, St Woolos school, with more suitable, heated rooms, opened its doors to it free of charge. Twenty-four children were taught there regularly with help from the Education Authority. Later a Welsh primary school opened in Risca. It existed long enough to celebrate its twenty-first birthday, and some of its scholars have become Welsh teachers themselves. After leaving Risca, pupils had to travel to Ysgol Gyfun Rhydfelen near Pontypridd, Mid Glamorgan, because there was no Welsh comprehensive school in Gwent.

By 1988 seventeen Welsh nursery and fifteen Welsh mother-and-toddler groups were scattered over Gwent. These children go on to attend Welsh units in six primary schools located at Newport (Highcross), Pontnewynydd, Pengam, St Dials, Bryn Mawr and Swffryd, with a total of

Janet Butcher of Newport carrying the *Corn Hirlas*
(Horn of Plenty) at the Proclamation in 1987.
(*By permission of the National Eisteddfod of Wales.*)

562 pupils in 1986, a number which has been steadily increasing. In October 1987, inspectors visited St Dials school Welsh unit and, in their report, praised the way in which it was run. In reality there are two separate schools on the site — the Welsh school and the English. The Welsh school totally immerses its pupils in Welsh, with the result that, although many of them come from English-speaking homes, they can communicate with each other fluently and naturally in Welsh. What is remarkable is that the number of pupils in the English units is decreasing while the number of pupils in the Welsh units is on the increase.

Children from the Welsh units in Gwent formerly went for their secondary education to Welsh comprehensive schools in Mid Glamorgan. Because of the increasing number of Mid Glamorgan children entering those schools, it has become essential for Gwent to establish a Welsh Comprehensive School, opening at Aber-carn in September 1988. It is significant that Aber-carn was chosen for its location, for Lord and Lady Llanover endowed the church there to hold its services in Welsh.

Gwent has its own Tutor-Organizer for Adult Learners based in the Underhill Residential College, Abergavenny. Forty-one Welsh classes are held in twenty-five centres, scattered over the county, both for beginners and for those who have a good working knowledge of Welsh and 'have crossed the bridge' — *wedi croesi'r bont*. Some classes are held once a week; others, in three centres (Bryn-glas — Newport; Fairwater — Cwmbrân; and Ebbw Vale) after the intensive 'Wlpan' course. Once a month, a one-day course is held, at different venues across the county. Weekend residential courses are held for all grades in Underhill College. The programme has included talks about Welsh customs, a craft course in Welsh and a course in preparation for the National Eisteddfod. Other plans have included a learners' eisteddfod of Glamorgan and Gwent, and a Summer School in Cross-keys College. Provision for adults to learn Welsh is therefore extremely good, and the *dysgwyr* are taking advantage of it. The support forthcoming from Gwent Education Authority is indeed praiseworthy.

Many local societies have been established; *Cymreigyddion y Fenni* has at times ceased to function and then has re-established itself. At present it is once more a flourishing society. The students of Caerleon College have their own Welsh Society. The *dysgwyr* of Tŷ Rhydychen ('Oxford House'), Risca, and of Bryn-glas, Newport, have their *clybiau Cymraeg* ('Welsh clubs'). Parents of the children who receive their education through the medium of Welsh attend meetings of their own society called *Rhieni dros Addysg Gymraeg* ('Parents for Welsh Education') — in nursery schools and mother-and-toddler groups as well as in the primary schools units. The new Welsh Secondary School stands next door to the church at Aber-carn where services are held in Welsh and where there is a Welsh Sunday School. Senior Branches (*Uwchadrannau*) of *Urdd Gobaith Cymru* have been established at Pontllan-fraith, Pontypool and Newport. The Youth Sub-Committee — *Blas Cas* — of the 1988 National Eisteddfod held many functions for young people *i godi hwyl* ('to have fun'). Teams of *dysgwyr* competed with each other and held various activities to raise money for the 1988 Eisteddfod. There is certainly a great deal going on so that Welsh speakers and *dysgwyr* can communicate in Welsh on all kinds of subjects.

Newport has a branch of *Merched y Wawr*, a women's movement which has branches all over Wales. Learners are invited to attend and are always given a warm welcome. *Merched y Wawr* should not be confused with the Women's Institute — though the latter movement was also founded in Wales. Naturally, the members of both movements have the same kinds of interests; but *Merched y Wawr* conduct all their meetings and write all their minutes, correspondence and balance sheets in Welsh. In short, they do all through the medium of Welsh, in accordance with their constitution which expresses the aims of the movement as being to 'strengthen public education, and especially to promote culture, education and the arts in Wales through the medium of Welsh, for the benefit of women in Wales'. The movement also publishes a quarterly magazine: *Y Wawr* ('The Dawn').

Recognition of Welsh culture in Gwent is increasing. One important landmark is the renovation of Capel y Babell, Cwm-felin-fach, for use as a museum. Once the place of worship of the poet Islwyn, it now houses his memorabilia. The museum was officially opened in June 1978 by the Rt. Hon. George Thomas MP, then Speaker of the House of Commons, and the occasion was marked by a bilingual service and the singing of Islwyn's famous hymn, 'Gwêl uwchlaw cymylau amser'. Launched by the Islwyn Memorial Society, which came into being in 1968, the museum is intended to be a centre for Welsh culture in the area.

People realize more than ever the importance of Welsh, an ancient language with a long literary tradition. In a report in the *Western Mail* of 12 December 1987, the Rt. Hon. Peter Walker, Secretary of State for Wales, was recorded as having declared his commitment to the Welsh language. He called it 'a fabulous language . . . a language with an enormous store of literature and poetry'. He wanted to see it as 'a reviving and thriving language' and felt it his 'duty to see Welsh children and Welsh adults . . . encouraged to take advantage' of it. He added that he would 'try to come to conclusions to help the Government to have a successful programme'.

Gwent has always been part of Welsh cultural history despite fluctuations in the number of its Welsh population. A new beginning has been made in earnest and it has kindled hope for Gwent both inside the county and throughout the rest of Wales. The welcome afforded the Newport National Eisteddfod augurs well for the future. It is hoped that its influence on the Welsh cultural scene will be felt to a greater extent than that of any of the previous four held in Gwent.

According to an old Welsh proverb, *Deuparth gwaith ei ddechrau* (starting is two-thirds of a job); the ardent Welsh people of Gwent and their supporters have already started.

Ymlaen y bo'r nod! (Onward be our goal!)

News & Weekly Argus

Newport News

Blackwood News

Cwmbran News

Risca News

South Wales Argus

REACHES ALMOST 450,000 READERS IN GWENT!!